MIUT £2.95

ROMAN EXETE
FORTRESS AND TOWN

by

PAUL T. BIDWELL

EXETER CITY COUNCIL

1980

Published by Exeter Museums Service,
Royal Albert Memorial Museum, Queen Street, Exeter EX4 3RX

© 1980
Exeter City Council

ISBN 0 86114 270 5

Published with the aid of grants from The Department of the Environment and Marks and Spencer Ltd.

Set in twelve on thirteen point Times Roman by Impulse Phototypesetters Limited, St. Ives, Cornwall.
Printed by Dowrick Design & Print, St. Ives, Cornwall.

To the people of Exeter.

FOREWORD

This book is about the origins of Exeter; at the time of publication it is the only up-to-date and authoritative account of what we now know about this first and most crucial phase in the City's development.

The story of Exeter's origins as a fortress of the Second Augustan Legion, and of its transition, in about A.D. 80, to a regional centre of government within the Roman Empire, has only emerged with any clarity in the last nine years, largely as a result of the work of Exeter City Council's Archaeological Field Unit, one of the first excavation units to be established by a local authority. Since its formation in 1971, the Unit has received invaluable co-operation and support from the Department of the Environment and the University of Exeter. In particular I must mention Aileen Fox, formerly of the University, who initiated rescue archaeology in post-war Exeter and advocated the creation of the Unit. I know she has taken great pleasure in watching the results unfold.

The book is associated with the 'Exeter 1900' celebrations, both in their inception—it outlines the evidence for the foundation of *Isca Dumnoniorum* as a self-governing community in about 80—and in their execution: it is conceived as a real addition to our knowledge of Exeter's history and therefore to our enjoyment of the City. We hope it will be widely read and appreciated by everybody with an interest in local history and in the Roman period generally.

The author was for eight years a member of the Archaeological Field Unit staff and personally directed several important excavations, including the celebrated excavations in the Cathedral Close which revealed to our delighted eyes the legionary bath-house and the *basilica* and *forum* of the Roman town.

Stephen Locke, B.Sc., A.M.A., F.G.S.
Director of Museums and Art Galleries,
Exeter City Council.

CONTENTS

LIST OF ILLUSTRATIONS

PREFACE AND ACKNOWLEDGEMENTS

With the Roman conquest of Britain the long history of Exeter begins. A spur above the river Exe, uninhabited at the time of the conquest and never before occupied on a substantial scale, was chosen as the site for a fortress of the Second Augustan Legion in *c.* 55–60. From there the conquest of south-west England was completed and in *c.* 75 the legion was posted to a new fortress at Caerleon. After a few years Exeter became the chief town of the Dumnonii, an Iron Age tribe whose territory comprised Devon, Cornwall and part of Somerset. After conquest the tribe was granted the status of a self-governing community within the Roman Empire and from Exeter its territory was administered by the wealthier inhabitants. Although the town of Exeter was equipped with public buildings, metalled streets and defences, the effects of the Roman conquest in most parts of the Dumnonian territory can scarcely be detected.

During the first twenty years of its history Exeter played a part in events which commanded the attention of Roman historians. In 61 the Second Augustan Legion was summoned from its base at Exeter to join the army led by the governor of Britain against the rebels who had laid waste much of south-east Britain. The officer temporarily in charge of the legion disobeyed his orders; the consequent loss of honour suffered by the legion and the suicide of the officer added to the catalogue of disasters for the Roman government in Britain in the year 61–2. During the civil war in 69 the Second Augustan Legion at Exeter was responsible for securing the support of the other legions in Britain for Vespasian, commander of the legion when it campaigned in southern England during the years 43–46/7. Vespasian was victorious and no doubt the Second Augustan Legion now redeemed its honour after the inglorious part it had played in the stuggle against the rebels some eight years earlier. After the transfer of the legion to Caerleon, Exeter passes out of recorded history until the Anglo-Saxon period. For reconstructing the story of the Roman town we have to depend entirely on its archaeology; the mention of its name in Roman road maps and in a second-century Geography tells us nothing of its fortunes. The archaeology of the town is a matter of wall-foundations, floor-levels, wells and the rubbish associated with them—broken pots, coins and trinkets. These allow us to trace the physical development of the town and place its various stages within a broad chronological framework, but they cannot provide us with a great deal of information about the population of the town. Here we must turn to studies of similar towns elsewhere in Britain and on the continent.

This book was commissioned by the Exeter City Council to mark the nineteen-hundredth anniversary of the founding of the Roman town, and is intended for both the interested layman and students of Roman Britain. It draws on a long tradition of research into Exeter's past, but incorporates the results of excavations carried out between 1971 and 1979, many of which are unpublished. These latter have added much to our knowledge of Roman Exeter, and have been brought about largely by the establishment of the Archaeological Field Unit by the Exeter City Council. The Council has been foremost amongst local authorities in Britain in financing the excavation of archaeological sites faced with destruction by building development. Other bodies have also supported and helped to finance the work of the Field Unit, notably the Department of the Environment and the University of Exeter. Some of the results of these excavations are set out in this book, but it should be remembered that the recent work has also advanced considerably our knowledge of medieval and post-medieval Exeter. The full account of the excavations carried out by the Unit is to be published in a series of monographs, *Exeter Archaeological Reports,* two volumes of which have already appeared (see bibliography).

In the preparation of this book I acknowledge gratefully the assistance of many people. My greatest debt is to Christopher Henderson, director of the Archaeological Field Unit, for allowing me to discuss excavations which he has carried out in Exeter before their full publication, and for much encouragement, advice and assistance. I must also thank Mrs Francine Silvester for drawing some of the plans and typing most of the text; Miss Barbara Jupp, Mrs Penny Barber, Mrs Susan Hill, Wallace Widgery and Stuart Blaylock for preparing the remainder of the drawings. Eric Haddon drew Fig. 16, prepared the cover illustrations and made the model of the legionary baths. Some typing was also undertaken by Mrs Helen McNeil and Mrs Elaine Holden. The photographs were taken by Bruce Sinclair (Figs. 34, 35, 40, 46, 47, 49), Robert Turner (Figs. 12, 14, 15, 20, 31, 39, 48) and Nigel Cheffers-Heard (Figs. 8, 10, 13, 17, 22, 45). Mr. G. C. Boon suggested many alterations and corrections, greatly to the benefit of the text, and thanks are also due to four members of the Exeter Archaeological Advisory Committee, Mr Stephen Locke, Dr Valerie Maxfield, Professor Malcolm Todd and Dr C. J. Young, for their comments. I am also grateful to Mr Bob Silvester for information about Iron Age and Roman Devon, and especially for help in compiling Fig. 6; to Mr Norman Shiel for identifying the Roman coins from Exeter and discussing their significance with me; and to Mr G. B. Dannell and Miss B. M. Dickinson for providing dates for the samian ware and samian potters' stamps respectively. Miss Jane Baker provided a photograph of Fig. 1 and information about the painting.

A great many people have been associated with the excavations undertaken at Exeter since 1971. Overall control has been in the hands of Michael Griffiths and Christopher Henderson, successive directors of the Archaeological Field Unit. Stewart Brown and John Pamment are the supervisors who have been chiefly concerned with the recent excavations described in this book. Much encouragement and assistance has been provided by Mr Stephen Locke, director of the Exeter Museums Service.

Finally, it is necessary to record that the publication costs of this book were met by Exeter City Council, with the help of grants from the Department of the Environment and Marks and Spencer Ltd.

Paul T. Bidwell
Chesterholm-*Vindolanda*
Hexham, Northumberland.
22nd May 1980.

CHRONOLOGICAL SUMMARY

DATE (A.D.)	RELEVANT EVENTS IN BRITAIN	EVENTS AT EXETER
43	Roman conquest commenced	Site unoccupied.
c. 55–60	Conquest of Dumnonii undertaken.	Legionary fortress and supply-base (?) established. Port at Topsham?
c. 60–65	Rebellion of Boudica in 61.	Legionary baths constructed.
c. 65–70		Enlargement of supply-base (?).
c. 75	Second Legion in fortress at Caerleon. Garrisons withdrawn from South-West.	Supply-base (?) demolished. Fortress vacated and timber buildings demolished.
79–80	Dumnonii established as *civitas peregrina*.	Exeter becomes *civitas* capital. Construction of *basilica* and *forum* (and public baths?) commenced. Street-plan of fortress adapted to serve town.
79–80 to 180–200		The period of the early town. Legionary defences retained but evidence of suburban occupation. Domestic buildings within the town of timber; first stone houses at end of period.
c. 180–200	Clodius Albinus proclaims himself emperor in 196	Construction of larger defensive circuit consisting of bank (and stone wall and gates?). Street-system extended into newly-enclosed areas. Extensive alterations to *basilica* and *forum* (and public baths?).
Third century		Many houses erected in masonry, some of considerable size.
Late third century		Alterations to the *basilica* and *forum*. New street laid out in southern quadrant of town.
Mid fourth to early fifth century	Britain abandoned as a Roman province in c. 410.	Alterations to the *basilica* and *forum*, including extension of *basilica* and construction of tribunal.
Mid fifth century		Establishment of Christian (?) cemetery on site of *basilica* and *forum*, which had been demolished in the late fourth or early fifth century.

In the earlier part of this book chronological periods are often referred to by the name of a reigning emperor or Imperial house. Their dates are as follows:

Claudius 41–54 ⎤
Nero 54–68 ⎦ Pre-Flavian
(Civil War 69)
Vespasian 69–79 ⎤
Titus 79–81 ⎥ Flavian
Domitian 81–96 ⎦
Nerva 96–8
Trajan 97–117
Hadrian 117–138
Antoninus Pius 138–161 ⎤
Marcus Aurelius 161–180 ⎥ Antonine
Commodus 176–192 ⎦

I. THE HISTORY OF PREVIOUS RESEARCH

The legendary history of Exeter

In Geoffrey of Monmouth's *The History of The Kings of Britain* there is a mythical account of a siege of Exeter by Vespasian. Arvirargus, a British king, had refused homage to Rome, and Vespasian was sent by Claudius to impose the authority of Rome. Vespasian prepared to land at Richborough (now, in fact, thought to have been the main landing-place of the Roman army of invasion in 43), but was turned back by a large force and instead landed at Totnes. 'Once Vespasian was on dry land he marched to Kaerpenhuelgoit, now called Exeter, and prepared to blockade that city. When Vespasian had besieged Exeter for seven days, Arvirargus arrived with his army and attacked him. The armies of both contestants were badly mauled all that day, but neither gained the victory. The next morning Queen Genvissa acted as mediator and the leaders made peace. They sent their troops over to Ireland. Once winter had passed Vespasian returned to Rome, while Arvirargus remained in Britain'.[1]

This story mixes historical and invented personages and events. In 1586 Camden wrote 'I am so far from affirming with Geoffrey of Monmouth, that [Exeter] was taken by Vespasian . . . that I hardly think it was then built'.[2] But Hooker, writing in the late sixteenth century, repeated the legend.[3] He also took another passage from Geoffrey of Monmouth, where it is said that Brutus the Trojan, having wrested Albion from the possession of the giants, gave Cornwall to his companion Corineus,[4] and embroidered its theme, alleging that Corineus founded the city of Exeter 'which emonge sundrye his other names one is Corinia'.[5]

The resistance which Exeter offered to Vespasian's supposed siege was adduced by Hooker as the earliest instance of the City's unwavering loyalty to the Crown—a loyalty which was tested in the course of sieges by the Danes and Normans, and in the Prayer Book Rebellion of 1549: 'The people of this citie have been alwaies dutifull and obedyente to the King and his lawes';[6] and this loyalty, both in legend and history, gave rise to the City's motto *Semper Fidelis*.[7]

Early antiquaries

In *c.* 1538 Leland visited Exeter and found two inscriptions built into the city wall: 'There appere 2 fragmentes of inscriptions of the Romaines sett by chaunce of later tymes in the town waulle renewid on the bak side of this house sumtyme longging to the Blak Freres. One of them standith in a tower of the waul, the other is in the waull hard by the tower'.[8] It appears that the tower referred to here is that standing at the eastern corner of the walls, a structure of undoubted medieval date. Leland did not record the texts of these inscriptions. They are not mentioned by later writers and were presumably removed during a later refurbishment of the city walls. No other inscriptions have ever been recorded from Exeter.

The first extensive history of Exeter was written by John Hooker at the end of the sixteenth century. His account of the Roman town was confined to the repetition and embroidery of Geoffrey of Monmouth's legends, as we have seen (see above), and to speculations as to the origins of Rougemont Castle: 'It is strongly ditched rounde aboute and was first builded as some thinke by *Julius Caesar:* But rather and in truthe by the Romaynes after hym for they hadd theire recourse to it for theire defence, refuge and aboade manye yeres'.[9] A few decades later in Westcote's *A View of Devonshire in 1630* there appears a careful record of finds made by labourers working near Rougemont Castle: ' . . . certain bricks [were found] three feet deep in the ground, and under them a little pot of the same matter wherein were divers pieces of Roman coins, both silver and gold; the youngest of them was of Antoninus Pius . . . thirty of them came to my hands.[In this area was also found] . . . a fair ring, in which was a beautiful stone set and thereon engraved the true idea of Cleopatra with the asp at her breast'.[10]

When Stukeley visited Exeter in the early eighteenth century, the city was flourishing and had a rich intellectual life. The principal local antiquary was Dr. William Musgrave, who settled at Exeter in 1691 and practised there as a physician until his death in 1721 (Fig. 1). He published works on medicine, and also *Belgium Britannicum* (1719), a description of antiquities in the 'Belgic' parts of Britain. Stukeley[11] examined Musgrave's library, 'a very good collection of books, coins and other antiquarian *suppellex*',[12] and the collections of two other antiquaries, Mr Loudham, a surgeon, and

Fig. 1: The Exeter physician and antiquary, Dr. William Musgrave (1655/7–1721). The book on the table, which is entitled *Arthritidographia,* probably refers to two treatises on gout published by Musgrave, *De Arthritide Symptomatica* (1703) and *De Arthritide Anomala* (1707). Portrait by Thomas Hawker (1640–1725) in the Royal Albert Memorial Museum, Exeter.

Mr Reynolds, a school-master. All three collections included coins from the large late third-century hoard discovered in 1715 near St Catherine's Gate;[13] no doubt they also included other antiquities from Exeter. Stukeley[14] noted several traces of the Roman period: 'One arch of south gate seems to be *roman*. no doubt the walls of the city are upon roman foundations for the most part'. Some of his observations were more fanciful: 'St. *Mary-arches* church and St. *Stephen's Bow* by their names seem to have been built out of *roman* temples'. He also considered that the Norman house in Waterbeer Street was originally Roman, and also Rougemont Castle, which, he thought, may have been the site of the *praetorium*.

In 1779 a group of bronze statuettes was found in constructing the cellars for a shop at the corner of Broadgate (p. 81). These were published in *Archaeologia* by Jeremiah Milles (Dean of Exeter, President of the Society of Antiquaries from 1768 until his death in 1784 and a Fellow of the Royal Society). He noted that finds of pottery, bones and oysters were also made at the same spot. Apart from a few coin finds mentioned by Alexander Jenkins in *The History and Description of the City of Exeter* (1806) no further discoveries are recorded until Captain W.T.P. Shortt took up residence in the city in 1832.

A study of Shortt's work has been published by the late R.G. Goodchild (1947), and need only be summarised here. During the twenty-three years Shortt spent in Exeter large parts of the city were rebuilt, and a great deal of Roman material came to light, much of which came into his hands and was published in local newspapers, often at weekly intervals. The early articles were collected in *Sylva Antiqua Iscana* (1841), and he pasted articles which he wrote after that date into a scrap-book which is preserved in the West Country Studies Library at Exeter. They describe over 700 coins and 60 samian stamps, as well as various structural remains. Shortt was also the first scholar to discuss at length the exact nature of the Roman occupation at Exeter: he described the settlement as 'a winter Camp or station of the Romans' and published a plan of the *Castrametatio Romana Iscana,* based on Polybius' account of a camp in the *Histories* (Fig. 2). The result is only of antiquarian interest; for example, Rougemont becomes the *castellum arx* or *acropolis,* and the Norman house in Waterbeer Street is identified as the *praetorium*.

Shortt was also active in local politics as a Liberal. On one occasion this, together with his antiquarian interests, involved him in a court case. On July 3rd, 1835, he entered the site of the Upper Market, then under construction, in search of antiquities found by labourers digging foundations. The builder was Henry Hooper, a leading Tory and self-made man, 'coarse of speech and unpolished in manner'.[15] Shortt was ordered off the site by Hooper, who also threw a shovel of dirt at him. Hooper was found guilty of assault and fined 10s., although Shortt was upbraided for his 'warmth of temper'. The case caused a great deal of controversy, because it was thought that the Mayor and Court were influenced by political considerations in treating Hooper so leniently; the matter even came to the attention of Lord John Russell, leader of the Reform movement, who defended Shortt's position.

Shortt's activities as an antiquary also involved him in scholarly controversy. In his *Sylva Antiqua Iscana* (pp. 79–109) there is a section on 'Greek coins found in Exeter and its neighbourhood.' In 1837 Shortt had communicated a notice of these finds to the *Gentleman's Magazine,* but was rebuffed: 'Our Antiquarian Correspondent at Exeter has surely been grossly deceived. The idea of Greek coins having been found in such numbers is too preposterous to require serious refutation' (p. 450); however, later in the year the *Gentleman's Magazine* published an abridged version of Shortt's account (pp. 292–3) which had originally appeared in the *Exeter Gazette*. The Greek and other eastern coins from Exeter, which include Byzantine issues, have been much discussed, but in the light of modern knowledge it is impossible to accept their authenticity (see p. 87n.6). Shortt seems to have been fobbed off with material discarded from a coin collection; doubt must also attach to an Egyptian *sistrum*-head which he published (see p. 82). The motives for passing off these objects as site-finds from Exeter are not difficult to determine: Shortt paid those who brought finds to him and these payments were no doubt increased when the finds were out of the ordinary.[16]

Nevertheless Shortt's work is still of considerable value, and the greater part of his collection of coins and samian is now preserved in the Rougemont House Museum. His activities were also of importance because they established the practice of retrieving Roman and later finds from building-sites. In 1855 Shortt left Exeter and settled in Germany at Heidelberg, where he died in 1881, but his

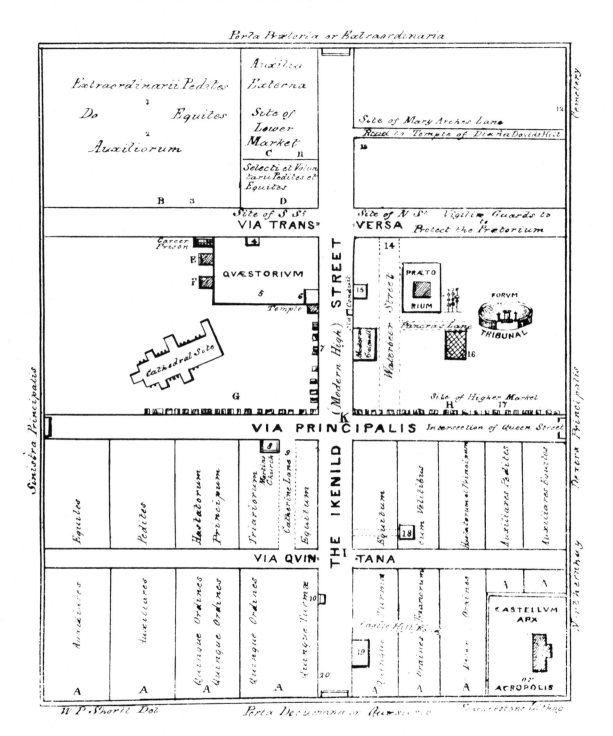

Fig. 2: W.T.P. Shortt's plan of the 'Station or Camp' at Exeter. The plan relies on Polybius' account of a Roman Camp and shows by means of numbers the location of various finds of Roman structures and objects (Shortt 1840, 'The Roman Camp of Isca', not paginated).

work was carried on by W. D'Urban and E. Parfitt. The establishment of the Royal Albert Memorial Museum in 1869[17] provided a repository for these finds.

Modern research

The Presidential Address to the Devonshire Association by R.N. Worth in 1891 is the first modern account of Roman Devon and Exeter. He discussed the archaeological evidence and historical sources, and concluded that the Dumnonii were 'a race numerous and skilful, civilised, well capable in numbers and in natural resources of self-defence, habituated to strangers, profiting by commerce. That race was never conquered [by the Romans]... There would be an acknowledgement of [Roman] suzerainty–little more than nominal; a certain rendering of tribute ... the periodical visit of a Roman trader—a welcome guest—or his constant presence in some favoured locality'.[18] Exeter was described as 'the final westward outpost of Roman civilisation . . . a frontier post and a fiscal centre'.[19]

Worth was wrong in concluding that the Dumnonii escaped conquest by the Romans, but his observations on the character of the settlement at Exeter are still valid (see p. 57).

In 1928 the Devon Archaeological Exploration Society was founded and at its first annual meeting an Exeter Excavation Committee was appointed. The programme of work for the Committee proposed by V.E. Nash-Williams, then Keeper of Archaeology at the National Museum of Wales, was extremely modest in its aims: 'so far . . . as the internal plan of Roman Exeter is concerned, the excavator may without qualms limit his efforts to the bare elucidation of the street-plan of the town, leaving it to the instructed imagination of the historian to clothe the skeleton with the habiliments of life. A few discreetly-placed diagonal trenches would give him all the information he needs, and incidentally should yield sufficient stratigraphical evidence to enable him to unravel both the origin of the town and the main phases in its later history'.[20] The first season of work took place in 1931, and excavations continued until 1938; some interesting results were achieved, including the discovery of a *piscina* associated with the public baths and the investigation of the town ramparts and walls.[21] Although the work was carried out on a very small scale, it showed that a rather more ambitious programme of work than that proposed by Nash-Williams would yield useful results.

In 1945–6 the clearance of war-damaged areas in the city provided an opportunity for excavations on a larger scale, which were directed by Lady (Aileen) Fox. The most important discoveries were made in South Street where a large metalled courtyard, now recognised as a market-place adjoining the *forum,* was found (see p. 52). Beneath this courtyard were sealed the remains of two timber buildings of pre-Flavian date, occupying a site near the centre of the legionary fortress, but originally thought to have been houses belonging to an early civil settlement. Further excavations carried out by Lady Fox during the next twenty years investigated the defences of the town and the South Gate, the public baths, houses and streets. Other work was carried out by E. Greenfield (p. 74) and M-J. Mountain (p. 66n.1).

Until 1964 excavation failed to produce any recognisable traces of early military occupation at Exeter. But in that year work at the South Gate revealed a short length of military ditch below the town rampart, and Exeter, like many other Romano-British towns, could be shown to have owed its origins to the presence of a military establishment in its vicinity.

In 1971 the Exeter Museums Archaeological Field Unit was established by Exeter City Council with support from the Department of the Environment and the University of Exeter. Excavations were immediately started on two important sites: the church of St. Mary Major in the Cathedral Close and the proposed Guildhall Shopping Centre. On the former site a substantial Neronian bath-house was investigated, and on the latter, timber barrack-blocks of legionary type and part of a workshop (*fabrica*). The existence of a fortress of the Second Augustan Legion underlying the centre of the Roman town was gradually recognised. Further excavations have recovered the outline of the fortress-plan and investigated other buildings. A great deal has also been learnt about the history of the later Roman town.

The future of archaeological research in Roman Exeter

Redevelopment has taken place on a large scale within the city walls since the end of the Second World War. During this period areas totalling about two acres have been excavated methodically, and salvage work has been carried out elsewhere (Fig. 3). At the same time the total area of

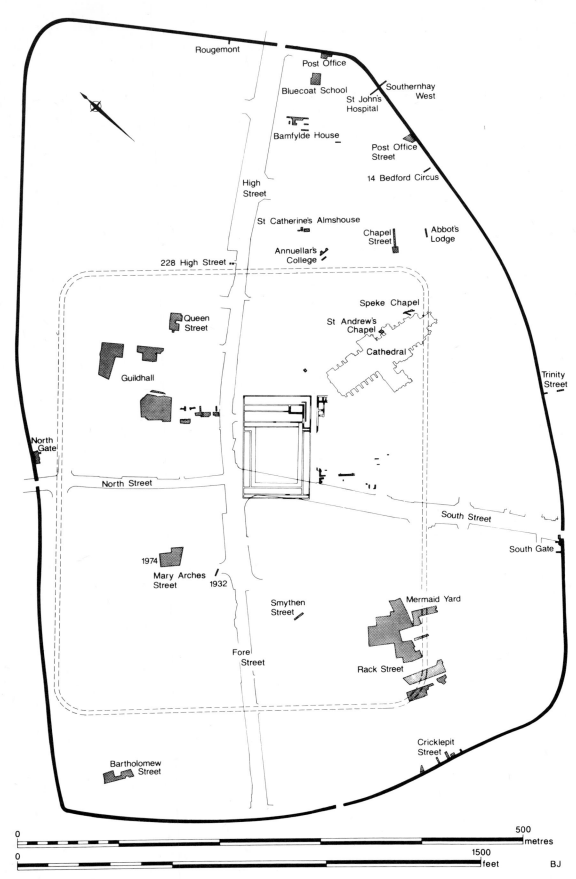

Fig 3: Sites excavated from 1929 to December 1979. The position of observations made in the course of building-work omitted. For the position of excavations on the site of the *basilica* and *forum* and the two *insulae* adjoining it to the south-east, see *EAR (i),* Figs. 4 and 22.

archaeological deposits which have been damaged or completely removed without record is very much greater because often excavation has been prevented by shortage of funds and time or sometimes refusal of permission for access to the site. Since 1971, more funds have been available for excavation, and the destruction of archaeological deposits without record has diminished. Indeed, in recent years the pace of redevelopment has slackened to some extent, and it has proved possible to investigate almost every building-site, although total excavation has seldom been possible.

Over the next few years rescue excavations within the walls are likely to be confined mostly to the south-western end of the city where large derelict areas are to be developed for housing. Work carried out in this area might be expected to reveal the plan of the fortress near the western corner and shed further light on the street-system of the Roman town.

There are considerable opportunities for research excavations. As much as twenty per cent of the Roman town lies beneath the Cathedral Close, gardens of the Bishop's Palace, the Palace Gate Convent and other properties near the Cathedral, and the archaelogical deposits are unlikely to have been much damaged by later activities. Only in this area is it probable that problems such as the development of the early Roman town and the character of the occupation at the end of the Roman period are likely to be solved.

NOTES

1. IV, 16 (trans. Thorpe 1966, 122).
2. *Britannia,* vol. 1, 36 (trans. Gough 1806).
3. Harte, Schoppe and Tapley-Soper 1947, 41.
4. I, 16 (trans. Thorpe 1966, 72).
5. Harte, Schoppe and Tapley-Soper 1947, 787. Hooker's editors point out (op. cit., 40–1) that the false attribution of this name to Exeter probably arose from confusion with Corinium (Cirencester).
6. ibid., 40.
7. The City's arms and title were granted by Elizabeth I in 1564 (Oliver 1861, 107, 208n.5).
8. *Itinerary,* Pt. III, Fo.33, Smith 1907, 228.
9. Harte, Schoppe and Tapley-Soper 1947, 41.
10. Westcote 1630, 39–40.
11. *Itinerarium Curiosum* (1724), 149. G.C. Boon suggests that the stone may have shown Nemesis spitting on her bosom; a representation of Cleopatra is scarcely likely.
12. One item in Musgrave's collection was the over-lifesize head of a woman with a Flavian hair style, which was found at Walcot near Bath in 1714 or 1715 (illustrated in Toynbee 1964, Pl. IXa and b, and in Cunliffe 1969, Pl. LXX). It was published as Tab. XV in his *Belgium Britannicum* (1719) and was a prized piece: '*hoc quod dono mihi datum, et in porticu nostra hodie propter raritatem muro affixum est . .* ' (p. 217).
13. See N. Shiel in *EAR*(i), 167–79.
14. *Itinerarium Curiosum* (1724), 148–51.
15. Newton 1968, 49–50.
16. Shortt wrote of these transactions: 'I retire highly gratified; they also, but from different motives: I that I have secured all the antiquarian treasures; they that [they] have got some modern British coin in exchange, to assist in prolonging their libations at the tavern' (*Gentleman's Magazine* 1836, 157).
17. Newton 1968, 186.
18. Worth 1891, 69.
19. ibid., 51–3.
20. Nash-Williams 1929–32, 9.
21. The results of these excavations and previous finds at Exeter were summarised and discussed by R.G. Goodchild in an unpublished thesis which was submitted in 1939 (copy in the West County Studies Library, Exeter; see also Goodchild 1946).

II. THE ROMAN ARMY IN SOUTH-WEST ENGLAND

Introduction

In recent years much has been learnt about the conquest of south-west England by the Roman Army, but the location of the Second Augustan Legion has long been a matter for conjecture, one strand of which has been fully vindicated—the suggestion that its fortress was at Exeter.[1] In this chapter the course of the conquest is considered in the light of the discoveries at Exeter. Its early stages are treated in a summary fashion, and the reader is referred to recent surveys.[2] The later phase is treated in some detail because the date at which the fortress at Exeter was vacated is unexpectedly late (c. 75) and requires consideration in the light of a critical examination of the evidence from other sites, particularly Gloucester, which has been claimed as a fortress established by the Second Augustan Legion in c. 66. In addition some of the other activities of the legion in the area, not all warlike, are described.

The South-West before the Roman Conquest

In the late pre-Roman Iron Age Devon, Cornwall and probably part of Somerset were peopled by the Dumnonii. Their political organisation and boundaries are of importance in determining the course of the Roman conquest of the South-West and must be considered here.

The only boundary the Dumnonii shared with other tribes was to the east where their lands bordered those of the Dobunni and the Durotriges. As early as the first or even the second century B.C. the distribution of metalwork and the existence in the South-West of a distinct class of small hill-forts with widely-spaced ramparts suggest the existence of a frontier area corresponding very approximately to the courses of the rivers Parrett in Somerset and Axe in Devon.[3] The evidence from the Roman period also suggests roughly the same location for the eastern boundary of the Dumnonii. Ptolemy ascribed a settlement at Uxela to the Dumnonii, and it presumably lay near the river of the same name which may be identified with either the Axe or the Parrett in Somerset.[4] The Fosse Way, which may mark the westernmost limit of Vespasian's campaigns against the Durotriges (p. 9), has been traced a few miles to the south-east of Ilchester and appears to be heading towards the valley of the Axe.[5]

The absence within their territory of very large hill-forts and of sites resembling the *oppida* of south-east Britain, and their failure to mint a coinage, may suggest that the degree of social cohesion achieved by the Dumnonii was less than that to be found among their neighbours to the east. This seems all the more likely when the size of the peninsula is considered: the distance from Land's End to the eastern borders of the Dumnonii is over 240 km (150 miles). Large tracts of barren upland such as Dartmoor would have separated populated areas. The effects of this are demonstrated by contrasts between western Cornwall, where tin-mining brought contacts with the continent and other parts of Britain, and more easterly areas; the population in the latter do not appear to have used pottery in the period immediately before the Roman conquest, while in western Cornwall a wide range of wheel-thrown pottery was manufactured (p. 41).

Differences in the culture and the basis of the economy in various parts of the Dumnonian lands, and the extended lines of communication, clearly made conditions less favourable than in south-east Britain for the centralisation of authority and emergence of kings. Cornwall and most of Devon lie within the Highland Zone of Britain, in the remoter parts of which Romanisation made little progress. Indeed, parts of Wales and northern Britain were garrisoned throughout most of the Roman period. Although there is no evidence and little likelihood of a substantial military presence in the South-West after c. 75, some of the Dumnonii may have been as troublesome as other tribes in the Highland Zone: and this may be one of the reasons why the early Roman town at Exeter was allowed to retain the defences of the legionary fortress (p. 57).

The conquest of south-west England *(Fig. 4)*

The Second Augustan Legion under its legate Vespasian (later to become emperor) was one of the four legions which together with a number of auxiliary regiments made up the Roman army of invasion in 43. Suetonius states that Vespasian 'fought thirty battles with the enemy, and reduced to subjection two extremely powerful peoples, more than twenty settlements *(oppida)* and the Isle of Wight *(Vectis)*'.[6] Mention of the Isle Wight places Vespasian's theatre of operation in southern

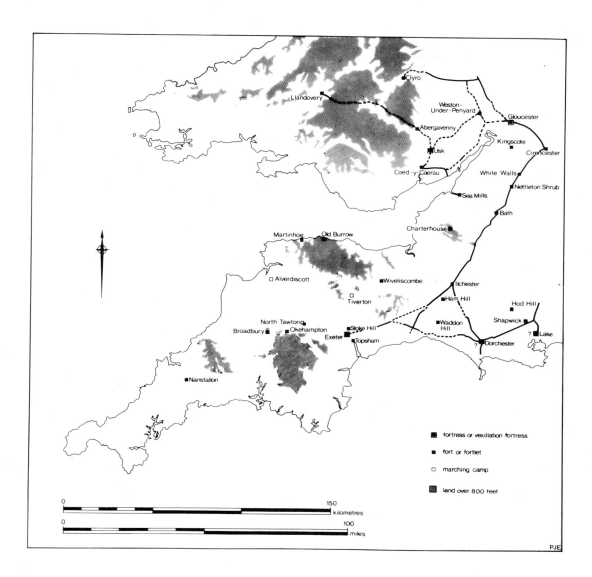

Fig 4: Certain and probable military sites in south-west England and South Wales established before *c.* 75. Principal roads also shown.

England, and there is little doubt concerning the identity of one of the 'nations' mentioned by Suetonius: at the Durotrigian hill-forts of Maiden Castle and Spettisbury in Dorset grisly evidence for the death in battle or massacre of the inhabitants at the hands of the Roman army has come to light; and at Hod Hill excavations suggested that the chieftan's hut had been singled out as a target for catapault arrows.[7]

The identity of the second 'nation' is uncertain, but it is unlikely to have been the Dumnonii because no military sites of such an early date are known within their territory (p. 10). W. H. Manning has proposed either a section of the Dobunni not allied to Rome or one of two tribes to the east of the Durotriges, either the northern Atrebates or a 'group occupying the Salisbury Plain area who were later incorporated in the *civitas* of the Belgae'.[8] Vespasian probably served as legate of the Second Augustan Legion until 46 or 47, and this would have allowed him three or four annual campaigns.[9] At about the time when he relinquished his command a frontier system was established along the north-western edge of Lowland Britain. This was based on the Fosse Way, a road which ran from the Humber into south-west England. Its course has been traced just to the south of Ilchester in Somerset, and, as already noted (p. 8), it appears to be heading south-westwards along the valley of the Axe. The lower part of its line, corresponding with what is usually taken as the boundary between the Durotriges and the Dumnonii, may have marked the approximate limit of Vespasian's campaigns.

Within the territory of the Dumnonii there are no military sites which can be shown to date from the reign of Claudius, although only one of the four forts known at present (see below), Nanstallon, has been investigated in detail. Nevertheless it would have been necessary to control the crossing of the Exe at Exeter at an early stage in any campaign which penetrated the territory of the Dumnonii; but at Exeter there are no sure signs of Claudian occupation. Present evidence would thus seem to indicate that the conquest of the Dumnonii was deferred until the reign of Nero.

In the years following the departure of Vespasian the Second Augustan Legion no doubt consolidated its hold on the newly-won territories. A number of early forts is known; but the garrison can only be deduced at Hod Hill, where there appears to have been a legionary cohort of six under-strength centuries (about 352 men instead of 480) and half of a quingenary *ala* (about 250–300 men).[10] Part of the legion may have been concentrated in one or more vexillation fortresses (p. 13).[11]

The governorship of Ostorius Scapula (47–52) saw military action in Wales which was continued by his successor, Didius Gallus (52–7). The latter is said by Tacitus to have 'pushed a few forts into the remoter parts, so that he could claim to have extended his sphere of duty'.[12] The foundation of the fortress at Exeter is most likely to have taken place during his governorship (p. 39). It would have been associated with an advance which would have eventually culminated in the annexation of the entire Dumnonian peninsula.

A number of military sites (see below) demonstrate the presence of a considerable force in the territory of the Dumnonii, and we may conclude that the tribe resisted conquest and that, in the aftermath, a network of forts was required to impose control; but of the progress of the conquest, and particularly whether the Dumnonii were subjected to Roman rule in the course of a rapid campaign or by successive advances over the years, there is as yet little evidence.[13] However, it may be that the events in 61 show that the South-West was not yet pacified. In the summer of that year Queen Boudica of the Iceni led a revolt which laid waste much of south-east Britain. The governor, Suetonius Paulinus, was in north Wales; when news of the revolt reached him, he summoned the Second Augustan Legion, but the *praefectus castrorum*, Poenius Postumus, did not obey the order. The rebels were eventually defeated, but Postumus 'stabbed himself to death because he had cheated his legion of an equal glory, and had disobeyed his general's orders in defiance of the traditions of the service'.[14] Postumus was third in order of seniority, and the fact that he was in command of the legion means that the legate and *tribunus laticlavius* were absent, perhaps serving with Paulinus in Wales together with a vexillation of the legion. A likely reason for his disobedience is unrest in Wales or south-west England.

The only possible evidence for warfare in the South-West during the Boudican rebellion comes from the hill-fort at South Cadbury where a massacre took place at the south-west gateway; brooches associated with the unburied bodies seem to date to this period rather than to that of Vespasian's campaigns.[15] W. H. Manning has suggested that the hill-fort lay within the territory of a tribe which had hitherto formed a client-kingdom allied to Rome: either a section of the Durotriges or the southern half of the Dobunni.[16]

Roman forts in south-west England

In recent years three marching-camps have been discovered in Devon by means of aerial photography; these are the only examples so far known in the South-West. Two, at Alverdiscott in north Devon (1.47ha; 3.6 acres) and at Tiverton (1.35ha; 3.35 acres), are of similar size. The third camp, at North Tawton, is much larger, at least 8.9ha (22 acres), and could have held, for example, a legion and several auxiliary regiments.[17] Four permanent forts are known but only one, at Nanstallon in Cornwall, has been extensively excavated. It appears to have been garrisoned by a *cohors quingenaria equitata,* an auxiliary regiment of about 500 men including some mounted troops.[18] A fort at Okehampton is about the same size and may have had a similar garrison.[19] About seven kilometres to the north-east at North Tawton there is another fort c. 2.6ha (6.5 acres) in area, including an annexe.[20] Two forts so close together are unlikely to be contemporary, and perhaps Okehampton, which produced a sherd of decorated samian dating to c. 70–85, is the later site. The fourth fort (c. 1.4ha; 3.5 acres) is at Wiveliscombe in Somerset.[21] Fortlets are known at Broadbury on the northern edge of Dartmoor[22] and on the north Devon coast at Martinhoe and Old Burrow.[23]

Auxiliary regiments in the South-West

Tombstones give us the names of three auxiliary regiments in the South-West:

(i) *RIB(i),* 159: the tombstone of a trooper serving in the *ala Vettonum,* which was found at Bath; it dates to the pre-Flavian period and is usually taken to indicate the presence of a fort in the vicinity rather than the result of an unsuccessful visit to the spa (p. 12).

(ii) and (iii) *RIB(i),* 108 and 109: tombstones of soldiers in the *ala Indiana* and *cohors I Thracum* respectively, found at Cirencester.

In addition there is a sculptured fragment from Cirencester which probably came from the tombstone of a cavalryman, and another possible tombstone from Whitcombe 3.2km south-east of Dorchester.[24]

These units lay within the probable limits of the area under the control of the Second Augustan Legion and would have come under its command.

The total number of auxiliary regiments in the South-West is unknown. A diploma for the year 103 supplies a list of units which, as E. Birley has shown, were probably under the command of the Second Augustan Legion when it was based at Caerleon: four *alae* and eleven cohorts, two of them milliary, are listed.[25] This gives some idea of the number of auxiliary regiments likely to have been attached to a legion, and thus to have been in the South-West at an earlier period. Indeed, two units mentioned on the diploma, the *ala Vettonum* and *cohors I Thracum,* were originally stationed in the South-West as we have seen above; the *ala Indiana* had been posted to Lower Germany in *c.* 80.[26] Four other cohorts, *I Baetasiorum, III/IV Lingonum, I Morinorum* and *I Vangionum* were thought by G. Alföldy to have been sent to Britain under Claudius or Nero, and it is quite possible that they were also stationed in the South-West.[27] The same may be true of a further six units mentioned by the diploma: of these, the *ala Pannoniorum Tampiana* is known to have been in Britain for at least some years before the end of the first century,[28] likewise the *cohors I Hispanorum;*[29] nothing is known of the whereabouts before 103 of the *ala Gallorum Sebosiana,* or of the *cohortes I Alpinorum, III Bracaraugustanorum* and *IV Delmatarum.* The other three units listed in the diploma were posted to Britain after the pre-Flavian period: *cohors I Tungrorum milliaria* following the Batavian revolt in 69–70,[30] and *cohors II Thracum* in the late first century;[31] *cohors I Cugernorum* was not raised until Trajan's reign.[32]

The military administration and exploitation of south-west England

By the late Neronian period the Second Augustan Legion controlled the territories of three large tribes, the Dobunni, the Dumnonii and the Durotriges. Certain duties would have been imposed on the population, notably payment of taxes and work on projects such as road-building. Little can be usefully said about these matters because such aspects of the military occupation can only be elucidated by inscriptions or by documentary sources, which are wholly lacking in the South-West. Members of the conquered tribes would have been recruited into auxiliary regiments; a tombstone from Cologne records a Dumnonian, Aemilius, the son of Saenus, who served in the Rhine Fleet.[33]

Tacitus observed that 'Britain yields gold, silver and other metals, the rewards of victory';[34] and there is a fair amount of evidence for the exploitation of mineral resources in the region. Roman exploitation of the Mendip lead-mines dates from 49 at the latest and a lead pig from St-Valéry-sur-Somme near Boulogne has a Neronian stamp of the Second Augustan Legion.[35] In the vicinity of the fort at Nanstallon (p. 10) there were deposits of silver-lead and haematite; small quantities of gold could have been panned out of nearby streams. Evidence from the fort demonstrates that both silver and iron were worked.[36]

Two sources of building stone of great importance throughout the Roman period were probably first exploited by the Second Augustan Legion. Purbeck marble was quarried in south-east Dorset; this stone, a partly metamorphosed limestone largely composed of gastropod shells, and not a true marble, is greenish- or blue-grey in colour and takes a high polish. It was in common use for tombstones and inscriptions, as well as architectural and decorative details such as mouldings or wall-veneers. The quarries were certainly in operation before 61,[37] and the stone was used extensively for the interior decoration of the fortress baths at Exeter, constructed *c.* 60–5 (p. 28).[38] Another important stone was Bath oolite, which was used for two pre-Flavian tombstones at Colchester, both found face down and probably overthrown during the Boudican rebellion; the tombstone of Rufus Sita from

Gloucester, also pre-Flavian in date, and the tomb of Classicianus from London, which dates to the early 60s, are also of this stone.[39] Smaller quarries were opened in east Devon to provide building-materials for the fortress baths at Exeter, although most of the stone was probably obtained from Rougemont just beyond the northern corner of the fortress (p. 41).

The Roman army provided an important market for the potters making black-burnished ware in south-east Dorset. Their products appear plentifully in the early military establishments in Dorset.[40] This industry was also the single most important source of coarse wares for the later fortress at Exeter (p. 41) and its products travelled as far as the Neronian fortress of the Twentieth Legion at Usk in Gwent.[41]

Some discussion of the extensive mineral spa at Bath (*Aquae Sulis*) must be appended to these notes on the peaceable activities of the Roman army in south-west England. It seems that the baths and temple complex were erected in the first century, although at present the construction-date cannot be fixed more precisely. In a recent survey the 'Romanizing phase of Agricola's governorship' was favoured,[42] implicitly emphasizing the civil status of the spa, but H. von Petrikovits has suggested that Bath was first and foremost a military spa.[43] From other provinces there are clear signs of military interest in certain spas: for example, at Aachen (*Aquae Granni*) many tilestamps of legions stationed in Lower Germany and of the Rhine Fleet have been found; and at Baden-Baden (*Aquae*) technicians of two legions and auxiliary regiments in Upper Germany erected buildings in c. 85.

There seems a strong possibility that the spa at Bath was established for the use of the Roman army while south-west England was under military administration.[44] Five of the tombstones from Bath are of soldiers, and one, that of a trooper in the *ala Vettonum,* has been dated to 'the closing years of Claudius, or to the reign of Nero at the latest'.[45] Most authorities consider that this tombstone indicates the existence of a fort in the vicinity. This may be so, but it may equally be taken as evidence for the pre-Flavian date of the baths. The military spa at Varaždinske Toplice in Croatia dates to before the middle of the first century A.D.;[46] and the construction of baths within the Neronian fortress at Exeter (p. 24) shows that at this date the Roman army in Britain was willing to undertake the erection of large masonry buildings and numbered craftsmen within its ranks who were suitably trained for the purpose.

The end of the military occupation in south-west England

After the rebellion of Boudica the Roman army would have found it necessary to strengthen its hold on southern Britain. This policy was successful enough to allow the withdrawal of the Fourteenth Legion from Britain in 66. Its fortress at Wroxeter was probably taken over by the Twentieth, leaving the fortress at Usk, it would seem, more or less empty but maintained until its demolition in c. 75.[47] Until recently it was thought that the Second Augustan Legion was moved to Gloucester at the same time; there, from a newly-constructed fortress, the legion could have continued to control the South-West while maintaining a strong presence on the eastern borders of the Silures. Recent excavations at Exeter, however, have shown that the barracks in the northern corner of the fortress were rebuilt after c. 66 (p. 40), and there are no signs of a diminution in the intensity of occupation until c. 75.[48]

The existence of a fortress at Gloucester, established after c. 64, is nevertheless certain (see below), and some explanation must be found for an apparently simultaneous occupation at Gloucester and Exeter before c. 75. V.A. Maxfield has recently suggested that the Second Augustan Legion may have been divided between the two fortresses and brigaded with auxiliaries.[49] There is no evidence to support this hypothesis. The identity of the garrison at Gloucester is unknown,[50] and although both fortresses are smaller than is usual, this does not necessarily mean they accommodated less than a full legion (p. 21).[51] In addition, no auxiliary weapons or fittings have been recognised from Exeter, and none is published from Gloucester.

The Second Augustan Legion, as V.A. Maxfield notes, is frequently said to have been divided during the first decade or so after the conquest, and legionaries are claimed as part of the garrisons at Hod Hill, Lake Farm near Wimborne, and Waddon Hill.[52] Dr. Maxfield also considered that two tombstones from Wotton near Gloucester, one of a trooper in *cohors VI Thracum* and the other of a soldier in the Twentieth Legion, hinted at a mixed garrison for Kingsholm, an earlier fort or fortress of unknown extent about a kilometre north-west of Gloucester.[53] But these two units may have occupied separate bases in the vicinity of Gloucester. A possible parallel exists at Colchester. The two well-known tombstones of Longinus, a cavalryman in the *ala I Thracum,* and of M. Favonius Facilis, a centurion of the Twentieth Legion, were found about 55m apart and came from a military cemetery which was probably wrecked in the Boudican rebellion.[54] The cemetery lay between the fortress under the *colonia,* garrisoned between *c.* 43 and 49 by the Twentieth Legion, and a newly-discovered fort at Gosbecks, four kilometres to the south-west. The latter, which has an area of 2.2ha (5.5 acres) is thought most likely to have been established in *c.* 43 and held for only a short time, although no excavations have yet taken place on the site.[55] It was large enough to have accommodated the *ala I Thracum.*[56]

Nevertheless, there is in Britain a group of first-century defended sites with an area of about twenty to thirty acres (8–12ha) which are claimed to have served as vexillation-fortresses, 'winter-quarters (*hiberna*) for battle-groups made up in varying proportions of legionary and auxiliary troops'[57] although some were perhaps stores-bases. About a dozen are known, but only the site at Longthorpe has been excavated on a substantial scale; it produced evidence for a mixed garrison, and was probably occupied between 44–8 and 61–2.[58] Auxiliary troops on occasions may also have been brigaded with a full legion. H. von Petrikovits has argued that a row of buildings in the *praetentura* at Novaesium, originally interpreted as accommodation for legionary cavalry, in fact represented the barracks for a quingenary unit of auxiliaries, probably an *ala.*[59]

The possibility that Exeter and Gloucester had mixed garrisons must be borne in mind, but there is another possible way in which their simultaneous occupation can be explained. M. Hassall and J. Rhodes have suggested that the Kingsholm site was abandoned entirely in 67 following the withdrawal of the Fourteenth Legion from Britain and the consequent redisposition of garrisons.[60] They attribute the establishment of a fortress on the later *colonia* site to the Second Augustan Legion which was withdrawn from 'its base in the South-West' (i.e. Exeter) in 69 when the number of legions was increased to four by the return of the Fourteenth. In the light of continued occupation of the fortress at Exeter down to *c.* 75 this hypothesis fails, but the events of 69 may point to a solution of the problem under consideration.

In the civil war of that year the British legions supported Vitellius against Otho and sent vexillations 8,000 strong to join his army. Otho was defeated at the Battle of Bedriacum; part of his army was formed by the Fourteenth Legion, which did not acknowledge defeat, claiming that only its advance party had taken part in the battle. The disaffected legion was ordered back to Britain but while it was temporarily stationed at Turin fighting broke out and 'on the night of their departure the legionaries left fires alight here and there, and a part of the *colonia* of Turin was burnt down'.[61] The legion remained in Britain only until the following year when it was sent to the Rhineland. Various locations have been proposed for its stay when it returned to Britain, most recently the fortress at Usk,[62] although G. Webster's suggestion[63] that it was temporarily brigaded with the Twentieth at Wroxeter should be borne in mind because the legate of this legion, Roscius Coelius, was a Vitellian and the *de facto* governor of Britain, the army having driven out Trebellius Maximus.[64] A further possibility is that the Fourteenth constructed and garrisoned the fortress at Gloucester. As already noted, excavation has demonstrated that the fortress was established after *c.* 64,[65] and it seems feasible for its earth defences and timber buildings to have been constructed within a year: a comparable site is Inchtuthil, where the defences and much of the accommodation had been completed in the course of perhaps as little as two seasons of work, and refacing of the rampart in stone had been started.[66] The employment of soldiers on various types of building-work was a device often used to enforce military discipline,[67] and the construction of a fortress at Gloucester would have absorbed the energy of the Fourteenth, the most troublesome amongst the legions which had opposed Vitellius.

This account of the origins of Gloucester is hardly compatible with recently held views about its early history.[68] Recent excavations have explored barrack-blocks in the *latera praetorii* which were occupied until at least 77–8, the date of the latest coins from occupation layers.[69] After *c.* 87 new buildings were erected on the site; their plans were very similar in outline to those of the earlier buildings, although the arrangement of the internal divisions was quite different. It was considered that this reconstruction was contemporary with the foundation of the *colonia,* which is thought to have occurred during the reign of Nerva (96–8). The evidence for the foundation-date depends entirely on an inscription from Rome on the tombstone of a *frumentarius*:[70] it appears to give the title of the *colonia* as *Ner(via) Glev(ensis)* or *Ner(viana) Glev(ensium)*. *Ner(via)* or *Ner(viana)* has been taken to represent an imperial epithet in the title of the *colonia*, signifying its foundation during the reign of Nerva or possibly later. Other inscriptions only give the title *Glevensis* or *Glevensium*: for example, the tombstone of a decurion from Bath or the well-known series of RPG *(R(es) P(ublica) G(levensis))* tile-stamps.[71] However, E. Phillips has shown that the inscription from Rome cannot 'be used by itself as conclusive proof that the *colonia* was a Nervian foundation'.[72]

There is thus no conclusive epigraphic evidence for the foundation-date of the *colonia* and we must fall back on the archaeology of Gloucester. At first sight this suggests a date after *c.* 87, when new buildings replaced the barrack-blocks. But excavations at Colchester have shown that parts of the barrack-blocks in the earlier fortress survived in use after the *colonia* was founded in 49, and, although the defences had been levelled, were still standing at the time of the Boudican rebellion in 61.[73] Perhaps the early colonists at Gloucester likewise made use of the fortress buildings down to at least 77–8 (see above). The foundation of a *colonia* at Gloucester in the early Flavian period would have promoted the Romanisation of the Severn valley and, perhaps more important in the short term, would have formed a bulwark against the Silures—another *subsidium adversus rebelles,* as in Tacitus' description of the role of the *colonia* at Colchester.[74] It should be added that a later date for the foundation of a *colonia* at Gloucester would make little difference to the argument. The early history of the town at Exeter (pp. 56–7) shows that a civil community could have established itself within the fortress at Gloucester, regardless of whether colonial status had been granted at the time.

The attribution of the fortress at Gloucester to the Fourteenth Legion and its subsequent transformation into a *colonia* shortly after the departure of the legion, while by no means proven, would resolve a conflict between the evidence for the late legionary occupation at Exeter and current views on military dispositions after *c.* 67. Occupation of the South-West must have continued on a substantial scale down to *c.* 75, although troops may have been spread more thinly after *c.* 67 when some of the territory probably controlled by the Twentieth Legion is likely to have been passed on to the Second. During the first few years of Vespasian's principate military effort was concentrated on the conquest of the Brigantian kingdom in northern England. Operations against the Silures were resumed in 74; southern Wales was rapidly overrun from bases already established as far west as the Usk, and even beyond in the coastal area, where Cardiff may now be included among the forts founded in the reign of Nero.[75] The Second Augustan Legion was transferred to a new fortress at Caerleon in Gwent where it was to stay until its effective dissolution in the late third century.[76] From Exeter there is abundant evidence for the demolition of the fortress and probable supply-base or stores-depot in the mid-seventies (p. 40), and, with the departure of the legion from the South-West, the period of military occupation ends.

NOTES

1. Frere 1967, 75.
2. Manning 1976; Maxfield 1980; Webster 1970.
3. Thomas 1966, 83.
4. Rivet and Smith 1979, 482–3.
5. Margary 1967, 123–4. It is possible that incursions were made into Dumnonian lands by the Durotriges in the years before the conquest (Fox 1973, 149–50). However, H. Miles (1975, 207) has suggested that the Durotrigian pottery from the hill-fort at Hembury is post-conquest. Comparison with other early groups of Durotrigian pottery bears this out (*EAR*(iv), forthcoming).
6. Suetonius, *Divus Vespasianus,* IV, 1.
7. K. Branigan (1974, 55) has raised the possibility that part of the Twentieth Legion was involved in the campaign, but his argument is not convincing.
8. Manning 1976, 26–7.
9. Eicholz 1972, 149–58.
10. Richmond 1968, 79–82.
11. Possible sites are at Lake Farm near Wimborne Minster where there appear to have been two successive forts *(Britannia,* 5 (1974) 455; Manning 1976, 21–2), and at Dorchester where opinion is divided as to whether a vexillation fortress could underlie the later Roman levels: Manning (1976, 23) does not favour this, but C.J.S. Green (personal information) thinks it possible.
12. *Agricola,* 14.
13. Manning (1976, 33) has argued that 'Nanstallon was founded late in the reign of Nero, certainly after A.D. 64', which, if so, might be taken to show that control of the western part of the Dumnonian peninsula was not established until as much as a decade after the foundation of the fortress at Exeter (cf. ibid., 40). The argument depends on the absence from the site of Claudian coins, both official issues and copies; these were in circulation during the first ten years of Nero's reign, when no fresh supplies of bronze coinage were minted in the West.
14. Tacitus, *Annals,* XIV, 37.
15. Manning 1976, 37–8. A revised consideration by W.H. Manning is to appear in the series of volumes *Report on the Excavations at Usk 1965–1976.*
16. ibid., 39.
17. Alverdiscott and North Tawton: Silvester 1978; Tiverton: King 1978.
18. Fox and Ravenhill 1972, 84–6.
19. Bidwell, Bridgwater and Silvester 1979.
20. St. Joseph 1958, 98.
21. Webster 1959.
22. Fox 1974, 91.
23. Fox and Ravenhill 1966.
24. Cirencester: Griffiths 1978, 396–7; Dorchester: Farrar 1965, where, however, it is thought that the relief may portray a rider-hero or hunter-god, and it is observed that the bearded face, if that of a cavalryman, should indicate a date in the second century.

25. *CIL* XVI, 48; Birley 1952, 18–9.
26. Certainly some time after the Batavian revolt in 69 (*cf.* Frere 1978, III.n.1) because it does not appear on a diploma of 78 which apparently gives a full list of the *alae* then stationed in Lower Germany (Alföldy 1968, 19, 152–3).
27. ibid., 86.
28. Frere 1978, 162n.4; Saxer 1967, 24–5.
29. Alföldy 1968, 42, 190.
30. ibid., 73.
31. ibid., 71.
32. ibid., 84.
33. *Aemilio Saeni f(ilius) mil(iti) ex classe G(ermanica) P(ia) F(ideli) pl(eromate) Euhodi n(avarchi) civi Dumnonio an(norum) . . . . .* *A E* (1956), no 249; Birley 1979, 104, 189); he may well have been recruited after the military occupation of the South-West came to an end.
34. Tacitus, *Agricola,* 12.
35. *CIL* VII, 1201, XIII, 3491; Elkington 1976, 183, 230.
36. Fox and Ravenhill 1972, 90–1, 108–11.
37. Purbeck marble has been found in a context dating to *c.* 55–60 at Lake Farm, Wimborne (Beavis 1970, 194).
38. *EAR*(i), 136–45.
39. Colchester: *RIB*(i), 200, 201; Gloucester: *RIB*(i), 121, L. Richardson in Rhodes 1964, 10; London:*RIB*(i), 12, Williams 1971, 95.
40. Hod Hill: Richmond 1968, 58–9; Waddon Hill: Webster 1960, 93; Lake Farm, Wimborne: Darling 1977, 67.
41. Greene 1973, 33. G. C. Boon thinks it not unlikely that the Second Augustan Legion was responsible for the importation of this ware to the northern frontier in the early Hadrianic period (*Archaeol. Cambrensis,* 123 (1974) 185).
42. Cunliffe 1969, 129. A recent study by T.F.C. Blagg (1979) of architectural elements from the adjoining Temple of Sulis Minerva suggests a construction-date as early as the Neronian or early Flavian period (i.e. within the period of military occupation in the South-West).
43. Von Petrikovits 1968, 91.
44. Provision of a spa by the Roman army for its own use would not exclude civilian visitors or the presence of a civilian community, both amply attested at Bath. Building inscriptions and altars dedicated by persons of known status comprise six by soldiers (*RIB*(i), 139, 143, 144, 146, 147, 152) and seven by civilians (ibid., 138, 140, 149–151. 153. *J. Roman Stud.* 56 (1966) 217); tombstones, four military (ibid., 156–8, 160) in addition to that of the trooper in the *ala Vettonum* (RIB(i), 159) and six civilian (ibid., 155, 161–5). Another example of civilian use of a military establishment can be seen within the fortress at Vindonissa, where a shrine for the offerings of ordinary soldiers has recently been recognised (von Gonzenback 1976), these being debarred from making use of the shrine in the *principia;* offerings were also made by civilians in the same place.
45. Birley 1952, 12.
46. Von Petrikovits 1968, 89.
47. Manning 1976, 41.
48. *EAR*(i), 16, 19.
49. Maxfield 1980, 303.

50. Maxfield (ibid., 302) points out that although no examples of dolphin antefixes from the Exeter/Caerleon mould (p. 23) have been found at Gloucester, triangular antefixes decorated with palm leaves are known and these can be compared with examples from Caerleon (Hassall and Rhodes 1974, 80, Fig. 31, no.1, palm leaves only; Boon 1972, Fig. 14, palm leaves framing a head). These antefixes are fairly common types and can have no bearing on the identity of the garrison at Gloucester.
51. While accepting that the barrack-blocks in the northern corner of the fortress are legionary (p. 35), Maxfield notes that their small size, when compared with other legionary barracks, signified that 'the troops were illiberally provided for or they were not all present' and finds the latter more likely if the legion was divided between two fortresses. But such a division would surely be effected by separating the legion century by century or cohort by cohort, and not by posting men from individual centuries to a different fortress.
52. Legionary armour-fittings and weapons have been recovered from these sites. It is possible that legionary equipment was issued to auxiliaries at this period (Frere and St. Joseph 1974, 39–40); for example, fittings from the *lorica segmentata* and helmets of Weisenau and Hagenau type have been found in auxiliary forts in Germany (Ulbert 1969, 14).
53. *RIB*(i), 121, 122; for the site, see Hurst 1975.
54. *RIB*(i), 200, 201; for the cemetery, see Hull 1958, 254, Pl. XLIII.
55. Wilson 1977.
56. Benwell and South Shields, which may have been planned for *alae quingenariae,* were 2.27ha (5.5 acres) and 2.08ha (5 acres) in area respectively (Breeze and Dobson 1974, 16–7).
57. Frere 1974, 6, Fig.3.
58. ibid., 36–8.
59. Von Petrikovits 1975, 55–7.
60. Hassall and Rhodes 1974, 31.
61. Tacitus, *Histories,* II, 66.
62. Manning 1976, 41.
63. Webster 1969, 277n. 1.
64. Tacitus, *Histories,* I, 60.
65. Hurst 1972, 50; Hassall and Rhodes 1974, 21.
66. Ogilvie and Richmond 1967, 74.
67. There is no clearer example of this than the treatment of the Thirteenth Legion, also part of Otho's defeated army, which was ordered by Vitellius to build amphitheatres at Cremona and Bononia (Tacitus, *Histories,* II, 67).
68. Hurst 1976.
69. ibid., 65; Hassall and Rhodes 1974, 21.
70. *CIL* VI, 3346.
71. Bath: *RIB*(i), 161; RPG: Clifford 1955.
72. Phillips 1978, 76–7. The relevant part reads *M(arco) Ulpio Ner/Quinto Glevi* and the element *Ner . . .* may stand for one of Ulpius' cognomina or his patronymic; *Ner . . . ,* if an epithet of *Glevi,* would more naturally follow *Quinto.*
73. Crummy 1977, 76, 81, Figs. 4 and 8.
74. Tacitus, *Annals:* XII, 32.
75. *Britannia,* 10 (1979) 273.
76. Boon 1972, 64–6.

III. THE LEGIONARY FORTRESS

The Roman name of Exeter

Isca, the name of the Roman fortress and later town at Exeter, appears to be a Latin rendering of the Celtic *ĭscā,* probably meaning 'water', in the sense of 'river'.[1] Although not yet attested epigraphically, it appears in various ancient writings. The earliest of these, Ptolemy's *Geography,* which dates to the mid second century A.D., is of particular interest because it places the Second Augustan Legion at Exeter.[2] The legion, in fact had been stationed at Caerleon in South Wales since *c.* 75, so that this was clearly a mistake on Ptolemy's part. Both Exeter and Caerleon are called *Isca,* and it is thought that Ptolemy, who omitted *Isca*-Caerleon from his *Geography,* placed the legion at *Isca*-Exeter, the only *Isca* known to his sources.[3] Since 1971, however, the remains of a legionary fortress occupied from *c.*55–60 to *c.* 75, which can be attributed to the Second Augustan Legion independently of Ptolemy, have come to light at Exeter. Although Ptolemy had some up-to-date knowledge about the disposition of the legions in Britain, which allowed him to place the Sixth Legion correctly at York for example, much of his information about southern Britain dates to the Claudio-Neronian period;[4] it is possible that this early source placed the Second Augustan Legion at *Isca*-Exeter and that Ptolemy saw no reason to amend it.[5] Exeter is also mentioned in the Antonine Intinerary, the final form of which seems to date to the late third century, where it appears as *Isca Dumnoniorum,* having acquired the tribal epithet which denotes its status as a *civitas* capital.[6] It also appears in this form in the Peutinger Table, which appears to date back to fourth-century originals.[7] Finally, in the Ravenna Cosmography, compiled in the late seventh century, the name appears in the garbled form *Scadum Namorum.*[8]

The *civitas Dumnoniorum* is attested by two building-stones on Hadrian's Wall, one found near the fort of Carvoran the other on the Wall near Thirlwall Castle;[9] these record the work of corvées, but their exact date has yet to be established.[10]

The site of the fortress

The fortress occupied a spur overlooking the River Exe, about 6.5km (4 miles) above its tidal estuary. Immediately to the north-east and south-west there are cliffs above the Exe, but the spur slopes steeply down to a level area between them, which may have been marshland in Roman times and where until the eighteenth century there was a ford just below the site of the early thirteenth-century Exe Bridge.[11]

The spur which the fortress occupied is easily defensible. Indeed, it has been suggested that the Roman occupation succeeded a hill-fort,[12] but this now seems unlikely; although traces of earlier occupation have been found, notably two hut-circles below the legionary workshop (see Fig. 20), and a prehistoric trackway crossing the spur down to the ford may have existed, no traces of defensive works have been encountered. As a site for the legionary fortress, the spur had a considerable disadvantage: the ground encompassed by the defences was sloping, and at the southern corner fell away quite steeply towards the river. As noted elsewhere (see p. 20), the fortress is exceptionally small, and this may partly result from the topography of the site, the construction of a larger defensive circuit having been prevented by very steep slopes, especially on the south- and north-western sides.[13] Nevertheless in the minds of the general and his staff who chose the site, its restricted nature must have been far outweighed by its strategic importance.

In recent years aerial photography and field-work have detected many single- and double-ditched enclosures in the Exe Valley and its surroundings (Fig. 6). They have yet to be satisfactorily dated by excavation, but they represent a type of native settlement, probably of Iron Age date, which may well have continued into the Roman period. If so, they would indicate that the Exe valley supported a considerable population at the time of the Roman conquest.

The plan, size and garrison of the fortress *(Fig. 7)*

Sections have been cut across the defences of the fortress on the south-east side and at the southern corner; a stretch of the later fortress ditch has also been recorded in the course of building-work on the south-west side of the defences (p. 23). Two partly-excavated barrack-blocks near the northern corner of the fortress (p. 35) belonged to a cohort-block, the plan of which can be restored with reasonable confidence, thus indicating the approximate position of the defences on the north-west

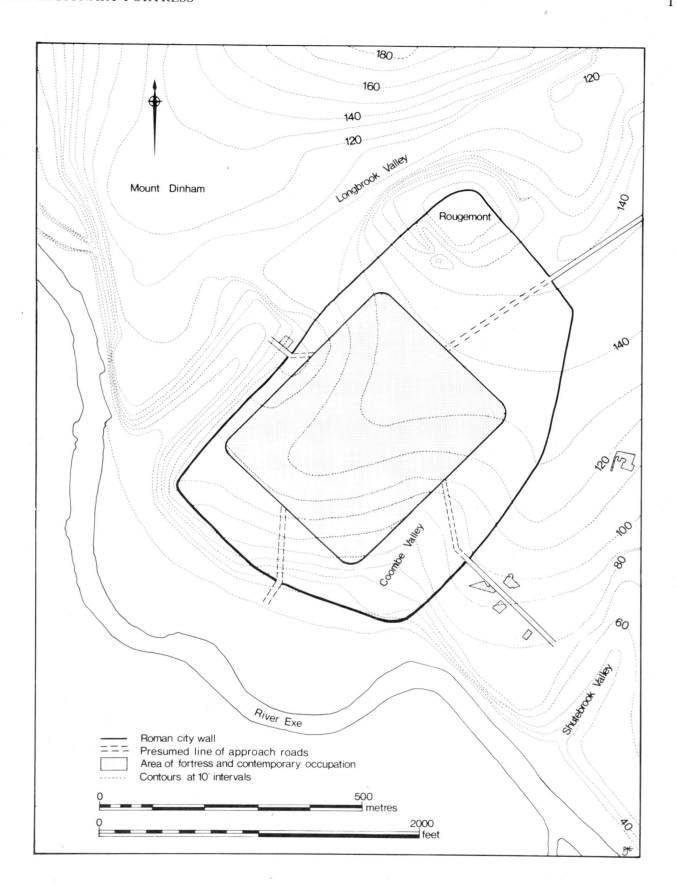

Fig 5: The site of the legionary fortress at Exeter with approach roads and areas where contemporary extra-mural occupation has been traced.

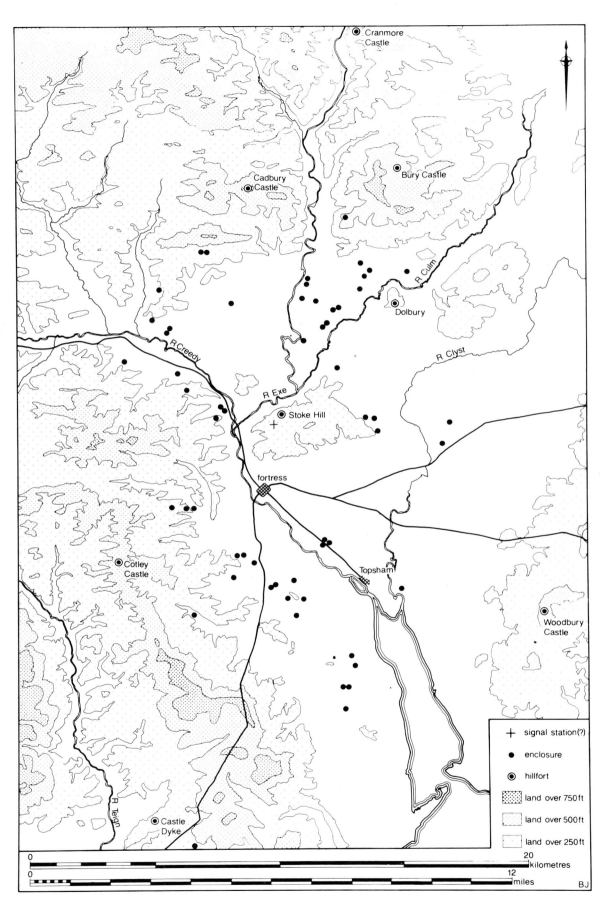

Fig. 6:

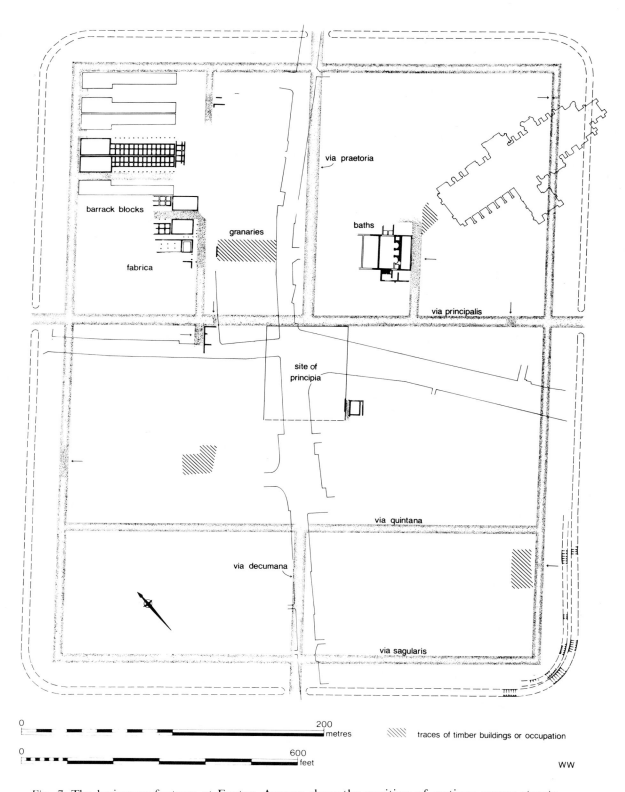

barrack blocks

fabrica

granaries

via praetoria

baths

via principalis

site of
principia

via quintana

via decumana

via sagularis

0   200
                                          metres

0   600
                                          feet

\\\\\\ traces of timber buildings or occupation

WW

Fig. 7: The legionary fortress at Exeter. Arrows show the position of sections across streets.

Fig. 6: Hill-forts and smaller ditched enclosures in the Exe Valley area. Both single- and double-ditched enclosures are shown. The settlements are likely to have originated in the Early Bronze Age, but many may have been occupied in the Roman period. The only excavated example (at Pond Farm, Exminster, see Jarvis 1976, 67–72) produced Roman pottery of probable late second-century date. The positions of modern roads which are likely to follow more or less closely the course of Roman roads are also included. Plan compiled with the assistance of R. J. Silvester whose co-operation is gratefully acknowledged.

and north-east sides. This allows the overall dimensions of the fortress to be calculated at *c.* 440m by 350m, measured from the conjectured position of the inner lip of the earlier ditch, giving an area of *c.* 15.4ha (38 acres).[14] The proportions of the fortress, length to breadth, are thus 5:4, as at Gloucester, Lauriacum, Carnuntum and Lambaesis.[15] The plan of the fortress seems best reconstructed as a parallelogram with angles of about 88.5 and 91.5 degrees. This slight deviation from the right angle is reflected in the alignment of streets and buildings; the only structure where the walls meeet at 90° is the legionary bath-house, constructed on a reserved site some years after the foundation of the fortress.

The width of the *praetentura* from the *via sagularis* to the *via principalis* is *c.* 160m, and that of the *retentura* and the *latera praetorii c.* 215m; this gives proportions of 1:1.35, rather less than the usual proportions of between 1:1.7 and 1:2.1.[16]

Much still remains to be discovered about the position of the streets and buildings within the fortress, but the main axes of the plan have been established. The *via principalis* has been sectioned at two points, establishing its alignment and also its width, which is *c.* 7.5m.[17] The *via praetoria* was seen for the first time in January 1980 at a point 32m from the estimated position of the *porta praetoria.* Several other minor streets have also been traced, but the courses of the *viae quintana* and *decumana* have still to be proved. In our present state of knowledge it is impossible to suggest the positions which such buildings as the *praetorium* (legate's residence) and *valetudinarium* (hospital) occupied, but some discussion of the possible arrangement of the barracks is called for. This is necessary because the size of Exeter (15.4ha; 38 acres) is a great deal less than the standard for many legionary fortresses, which is 20ha (50 acres) or more. This would seem to suggest that the garrison was less than a full legion: some cohorts may have been stationed elsewhere, as at Nijmegen in Holland (see below), or the legion may have been divided between two fortresses and brigaded at both with some of its auxiliaries. The second of these possibilities, which was put forward by V.A. Maxfield, is discussed on p. 12 f, where it is suggested that the disposition of legions in Britain after *c.* 67 does not necessarily require the Second Augustan Legion to have been divided between the fortresses at Exeter and Gloucester. The first of these possibilities, however, must be considered here.

Several legionary fortresses, dating from Augustan times to the Flavian period, are closer in size to Exeter than to the norm of *c.* 20ha (50 acres) or more: Nijmegen, 16.5ha (40.75 acres); Haltern in Germany, 16.7ha (41.25 acres); Lincoln, 16.8ha (41.5 acres); Gloucester 17.5 (43.25 acres).[18] Little is known about the plan of Lincoln, and not a great deal more of Gloucester,[19] but knowledge of the accommodation at Nijmegen and Haltern is sufficient to attempt estimates of their garrisons. In a recent survey S. von Schnurbein concluded that in the Augustan fortress at Haltern accommodation was provided for seven or, at the most, eight cohorts.[20] This is far from certain because the complete plan of the fortress has yet to be recovered, and C. Wells has argued that there was room for a whole legion;[21] he noted that in Augustan times the first cohort was no larger than the other nine, and thought that there was sufficient space for ten cohort-blocks, perhaps even an eleventh, when the unexcavated areas of the fortress were taken into account. At Haltern the barracks, which were *c.* 70m in length, and the *principia*, which measured *c.* 53.5m by 46m, are smaller than usual, and clearly 'scaled down', as at Exeter, to match the size of the fortress. At the Flavian fortress of Nijmegen, although rather less than half of the interior has been excavated, the general lay-out of the accommodation can be reconstructed; there is apparently space for no more than eight cohorts.[22] However, if Wells' estimate of the garrison at Haltern is accepted, it is possible that Exeter (and perhaps also Gloucester and Lincoln) may have accommodated a full legion, albeit in rather cramped conditions. At Nijmegen, it should be noted, the buildings were constructed on a somewhat more generous scale than at Exeter: the barracks were *c.* 72m in length (*c.* 62m at Exeter), and the *principia* measured *c.* 95m by 66m (*c.* 54.5m by at least 64.5m. at Exeter).

Turning to the plan of Exeter, we can take the barrack-blocks in the northern corner as a guide to the scale of the accommodation. H. von Petrikovits[23] has calculated that at Novaesium in Germany, Inchtuthil in Scotland and Carnuntum in Austria the accommodation for the whole garrison, including officers, made up respectively 67.5%, 76.3% and 79.5% of the area occupied by buildings in these fortresses. At Exeter, if the dimensions of the barrack-blocks in the northern corner are taken as the standard for the accommodation of all but the first cohort, for which we should probably allow the equivalent of two cohort-blocks, the area occupied by the barrack-blocks would

Fig. 8: Antefixes from the legionary baths. These would have been placed along the eaves of the building. The dolphin antefixes (nos. 3 and 4) were produced in the same mould as examples from Caerleon, a later fortress of the legion which was established in *c.* 75.

amount to 45.6% (5.6ha) of the area enclosed by the *via sagularis* (12.4ha). Even allowing 32.5% of the area, as at Novaesium, for other types of buildings, such as the baths, workshops, *principia,* etc., this still leaves 21.9% of the area for the residences of the officers (the *praetorium* and tribunes' houses), which is ample space.[24] At Exeter the scale of the accommodation would clearly allow for the presence of an entire legion.

The plan of the fortress, however, presents some difficulties. Barrack-blocks in legionary fortresses are most commonly arranged in three rows grouped into cohort-blocks: four across the *praetentura* on either side of the *porta praetoria,* two in the *latera praetorii* with the barracks of the first cohort on the right-hand side of the *principia,* and the remaining four ranged across the rear of the *retentura.*[25] At Exeter there seems to be sufficient space for a similar arangement in the *retentura.* In the *latera praetorii* a cohort-block would fit between the *via sagularis* on the north-west side of the fortress and the street which joins the *via principalis* at right angles opposite the *fabrica;* between the *principia* and the south-eastern part of the *via sagularis* there is a space *c.* 126m in width, sufficient to accommodate the barracks of the first cohort. In the *praetentura,* however, there is not enough space to accommodate the barracks of the remaining four cohorts along the north-eastern part of the *via*

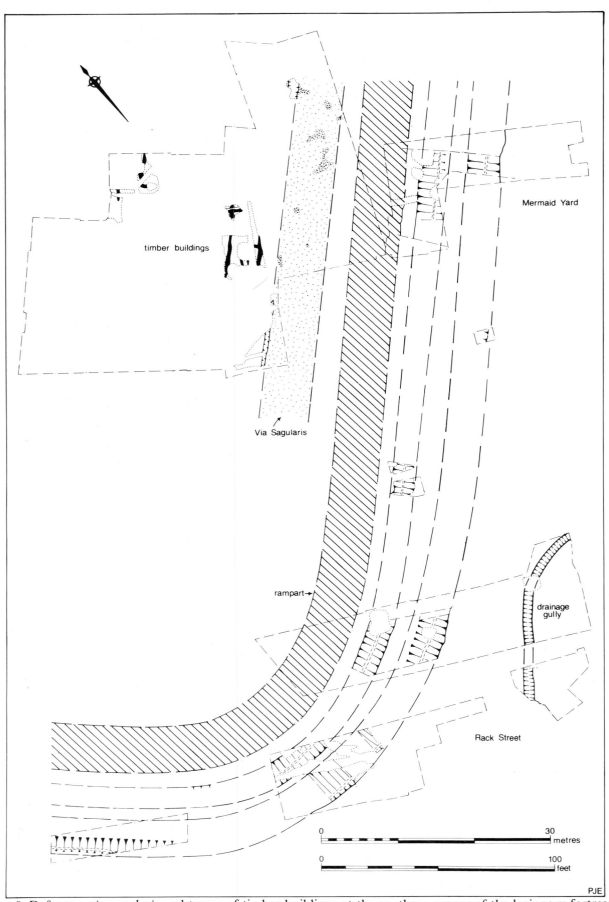

timber buildings

Via Sagularis

rampart→

Mermaid Yard

drainage gully

Rack Street

| 0 | | 30 | |
metres

| 0 | | 100 | |
feet

PJE

Fig. 9: Defences, *via sagularis* and traces of timber buildings at the southern corner of the legionary fortress.

sagularis. The cohort-block in the northern corner was probably matched by another in the eastern corner, but recent excavations have shown that there could not have been a complete cohort-block immediately to the north-west of the *via praetoria.* At a distance of 20m to the south-east of the cohort-block in the northern corner a narrow street has been uncovered. A sizeable area has been excavated on its south-east side, and can be shown to have been the site of at least two buildings during the fortress period which were certainly not barrack-blocks (p. 37). However, the cohort-block which was sought on this site may have lain elsewhere within the *praetentura.* The plan of Novaesium shows that the arrangement of barrack-blocks in the *praetentura* and *retentura* was not always as symmetrical as, for example, at Caerleon and Inchtuthil. At Exeter there is enough space for a cohort-block in the area between the baths and the south-east part of the *via sagularis.*

To sum up, in fortresses similar in size to Exeter accommodation was provided for up to eight cohorts, and even for a full legion, if Wells' interpretation of the plan at Haltern is accepted (see above). At Exeter, where the accommodation appears to have been 'scaled down' in size to a degree as yet unknown at other legionary fortresses,[26] there could still be sufficient space for a full legion. Accommodation for one or two cohorts may have been omitted. These could have been detached to form a vexillation serving elsewhere in Britain or on the continent.

The doubt concerning the size of the garrison at Exeter scarcely attaches to its identity. Contemporary historical sources make it clear that the Second Augustan Legion campaigned in southern England under Vespasian (p. 8).[27] Confirmation of the inference that it would then have formed the garrison at Exeter is provided by two antefixes from the legionary baths, which proved to have been made in the same mould as examples from Caerleon (Fig. 8, nos. 3 and 4). Presumably the mould belonged to a craftsman attached to the legionary tilery who took it to Caerleon as part of his stock-in-trade when the legion was posted there in *c.* 75.[28]

The defences *(Figs. 9, 10 and 26)*

During excavations carried out between 1975 and 1978 in Mermaid Yard and at Rack Street, the southern corner of the defences was explored (Fig. 9). The rampart, which was seen for the first time in Mermaid Yard (1977–8), was *c.* 6m in width and survived to a maximum height of 90cm (Fig. 26). There were no foundations, for example cobbling or a raft of timbers, and the rampart was constructed of compacted layers of clay with a revetment of clay blocks at the front. At Mermaid Yard there was a berm about a metre in width separating the rampart from a V-shaped ditch, *c.* 1.9m in depth and at least 2m in width, which has been sectioned at four other points along its course (Fig. 10). The ditch appeared to have been open for only a short time: there was only a shallow cleaning-slot as its base and its sides showed few signs of weathering. It had been filled with deposits of clay, which produced a small group of coarse pottery and twelve sherds of samian, the latest piece a Dr. 29 of *c.* 60–75. At a distance of 8m from the rampart a larger ditch was found. Four sections have been cut across it: in Mermaid Yard it was 3.8m in depth and 4.2m in width, but at Rack Street its depth was no more than 2.5m. The ditch remained open until *c.* 80.

The smaller inner ditch was apparently in use for only a short time and was presumably replaced by the outer ditch, although no stratigraphical link between them could be detected.[29] The modest dimensions of the legionary defences at Exeter can be compared with those of the fortresses at Usk and Colchester, both pre-Flavian foundations: at Usk there was a ditch only *c.* 3m in width, supplemented by an outer ditch, apparently of similar dimensions, on the south side of the fortress,[30] and at Colchester there was a single ditch 2.5–3m in depth.[31] The pre-Flavian vexillation fortress at Longthorpe in Lincolnshire was defended by two ditches, but these were fairly shallow: the depth of the inner was *c.* 2m, that of the outer *c.* 1.6m.[32]

On the north-west side of the fortress a V-shaped ditch, at least 2.8m in width and 1.4m in depth, was seen beneath the later Roman town wall at a distance of about 40m from the rampart. The course of the ditch ran towards the fortress defences at right angles (Fig. 24). The ground here slopes steeply down to the Longbrook, and it is clear that the ditch was not defensive. It was probably dug to carry water away from the fortress ditch which crossed a hollow immediately to the south-east. Finally, excavations by building contractors in a cellar in High Street,[33] just to the north-east of the fortress, exposed a section through Roman levels. Immediately above the clay subsoil a substantial layer of gravel metalling was found; this may represent a road or patrol-track skirting the later ditch of the fortress (Fig. 24).[34]

Fig. 10: The two ditches of the legionary fortress; section excavated at Rack Street in 1977. Between them can be seen the base of the civil ditch which was filled in the later second century (p. 46 and cf. Fig. 26). 2m scale.

The *intervallum* and *via sagularis*

The *via sagularis* on the south-east side of the fortress was exposed at Rack St in 1977; it was 5.5–6m in width and its position showed that the width of the *intervallum* was only 3.5–4m (Fig. 9). Another stretch at least 4m in width was uncovered in 1936 next to the Speke Chapel on the north side of the Cathedral.[35]

At Bartholomew St in 1959, on the opposite side of the fortress, the *via sagularis* was traced over a distance of 25m, and was found to have a width of at least 4m. The earliest levels in the *intervallum* on the north-west side of the fortress produced evidence for metal-working associated with coins of Claudius and Nero. Two or possibly three timber buildings were erected on the site in *c.* 65–70, and were destroyed by fire in *c.* 80–5.[36] They would appear to have escaped the general demolition of timber buildings within the fortress which occurred in *c.* 75, although it is possible that a re-assessment of the evidence for their construction-date, which has not been published in full, would show that they were erected after the departure of the legion, rather than in *c.* 65–70.

The legionary baths *(Figs. 11–18)*

The baths occupied a site *c.* 4000 sq.m in area in the eastern angle between the *viae praetoria* and *principalis;* they are much smaller in size than other legionary examples.[37] Only the eastern corner of

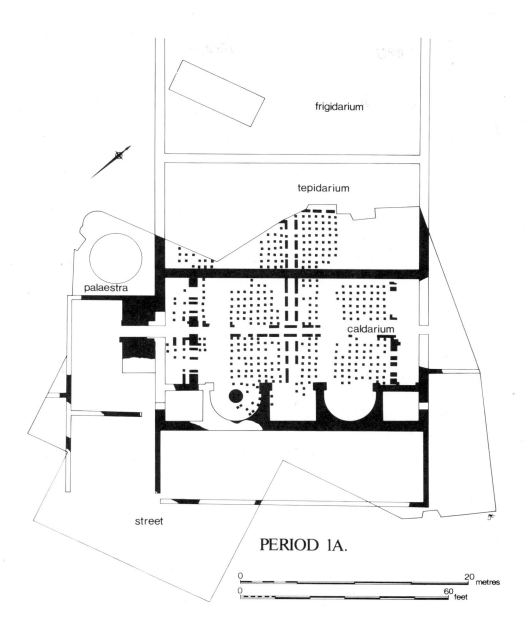

frigidarium

tepidarium

palaestra

caldarium

street

PERIOD 1A.

0   20 metres

0   60 feet

Fig. 11: Plan of the legionary baths before the alterations which took place in *c.* 75.

their site has been fully explored; the south-east end of the bath-house, comprising the *caldarium* (hot, damp room) and *tepidarium* (warm room), part of the *palaestra* (exercise-yard) and some of the service-buildings fell within the excavated area (Fig. 11). The *caldarium* was a rectangular room measuring 22.3m by 9.75m, on the south-east side of which were two apses flanking a central recess (Fig. 12). Two small rooms, which could only be entered from outside the bath-house, filled up the space between the apses and the side-walls. The two apses had a diameter of 4.7m, and an overall depth of 3.75m; in the centre of each apse at the level of the hypocaust there were circular tile bases which supported *labra* (water-basins). It is not possible to determine the function of the central recess; a small bath can be excluded because the surrounding walls, which survived to a height of 1.75m in places, were not pierced at any point by a drain. However, the recess was on the central axis of the building and may have housed an altar or statue (Fig. 13).

Two groups of tile-piers and *pilae* (supports for the hypocaust floor), occupying the entire width of the room at either end and spaced 40cm apart from centre to centre, instead of 60cm as in the rest of

Fig. 12: Legionary baths, interior of the *caldarium*. The two walls cutting across the south-western arms of the apses belong to the civil *basilica* which was built on the site of the baths in *c.* 80 (p. 49). 2m scale.

the *caldarium* hypocaust, supported baths *c.* 2m in width and 1m in depth. The hypocaust, which was served by two furnaces adjacent to the baths, was divided into four parts by two channels which bisected each other at the centre of the room; the channels were formed by lengths of tile-wall, the gaps between which were presumably intended to promote the circulation of the hot air to all parts of the hypocaust. This arrangement was also found in the *tepidarium* hypocaust. The tiles, 60cm square,

Fig. 13: Model of legionary baths. *Caldarium* looking south-east; to the right, figures gathered around the cockpit in the *palaestra.*

which supported the floor above the channels, themselves 60cm in width, were laid over iron bars; these rested on top of the tile-walls and served to strengthen the floor above the channels. In front of the furnace-flues the baths were supported by iron 'cages', the bases of which were embedded in brick-mortar under the tiled floor of the hypocaust-basement. The *tepidarium* was only partly excavated, but was found to have the same length as the *caldarium.* A possible clue to its width was furnished by the position of the longitudinal channel in the hypocaust. In the *caldarium* the channel which ran down the length of the room occupied its exact centre (excluding the apses and recess on the south-east side). If the longitudinal channel in the *tepidarium* also ran down its centre, an overall width of 11.25m would be indicated for the room. No traces of the presence of baths or *labra* were found.

North-west of the *tepidarium* a brick-mortar floor was revealed at the lowest level in a trial trench; this may have belonged to the *frigidarium* (cold room).

In the angle formed by the south-west wall of the bath-house and the *caldarium* furnace-house, a courtyard with a surface covered by compacted layers of sand was found (Fig. 15). This must have formed part of the *palaestra,* sited, as was usual, on the south-west side of the building in order to catch the afternoon sun. Most of the excavated area was occupied by a circular enclosure 4.4m in diameter; it consisted of a circle of timbers, each measuring 42cm by 11–12.5cm in section, which had been driven into the ground to a depth of 15–20cm. Their shallow depth of penetration suggests that the timbers could not have stood to any great height above ground-level. There is no reason to doubt that the circular enclosure was connected with the functions of the *palaestra;* that is, with the exercises and amusements of the bathers. It resembles cock-fighting pits erected in rural England and Wales a century or more ago, which were circular areas of level ground enclosed by board walls *c.* 30cm in height.

The south-west *caldarium* furnace-house measured 12.2m by 7.8m, and appeared to have contained a single boiler supplied by a reservoir (Fig. 16). The south-east end of the room was probably divided off to form a fuel-store.

Fig. 14:Caldarium hypocaust looking north-east showing the junctions of the two channels in the hypocaust. Right foreground, the steps leading from the *forum*-portico to the civil *basilica*, the south-west wall of which cuts across the hypocaust of the earlier baths at the rear of the steps (p. 51). 2m scale.

On the south-west side of the furnace-house a short length of wall was found; it may have been matched by another wall at the roadside to form a room 9m in width. Although there appeared to have been an entry to the room from the service-courtyard, its floor was at the same level as the *palaestra*. South-east of the furnace-house there was a courtyard (8.4m by 7.8m) opening onto the street which ran along the south-east side of the baths. An adjacent enclosure immediately to the south-east of the bath-house contained a row of four amphora-bases in its western corner. These presumably had been re-used as urinals; the liquid collected from them may have been employed in the preparation of leather or cloth. The area on the north-east side of the bath-house opened onto the street; a wall on its north-west side formed part of the north-east *caldarium* furnace-house, which lay mostly outside the excavated area.

A substantial quantity of decorative material was recovered from the demolition-layers of the bath-house and supplies much information about the appearance of the interior of the building. The floors were paved with white and dark-grey stone quarries perhaps arranged in chequer-board or simple linear patterns. Purbeck marble may also have been used for this purpose. Fragments of at least one figured mosaic, the earliest known from Britain, were recovered from the demolition-debris in the *caldarium* and *tepidarium*. The largest fragment shows two different subjects: above a plain band there is a circular motif flanked by two hoofed animals, and below, what appears to be a pattern

Fig. 15: The *palaestra* looking north-east with the probable cockpit (filling of the holes which contained the upright timbers unexcavated); foreground, north-west wall of the *caldarium* furnace-house; right, the robbing-trench of the south-west wall of the baths. 2m scale.

of leaves (Fig. 25,1). Part of a *cantharus* and an eye (?) appear on other pieces, but the majority are indeterminate or represent plain borders. D.J. Smith saw these fragments as 'the work not of a professional mosaicist but of a legionary craftsman uninhibited by conventional training'.[38]

Purbeck marble was used extensively for mouldings and veneers; fragments from a splash-board behind one of the baths and from a flight of steps have been recognised. The walls were no doubt painted, although little evidence of this has survived, and the rooms were lit by glazed windows.

The ceilings probably took the form of barrel-vaults, constructed from concrete and protected from the effects of the weather by tiled roofs (Fig. 17). Two types of antefix decorated the eaves (Fig. 8); by far the most common were examples portraying a human face (? female) framed by hair, but two fragments with dolphins flanking a rosette were also found (p. 23).

Perhaps the most interesting aspect of the building was its design. Unlike most contemporary bath-houses the building was apparently planned symmetrically about its central axis (Fig. 18). Its plan most closely resembles that of the early Flavian baths 'En Perruet' at Avenches, Switzerland, but can also be compared with the fortress baths at both Vindonissa, Switzerland (of Claudian date),

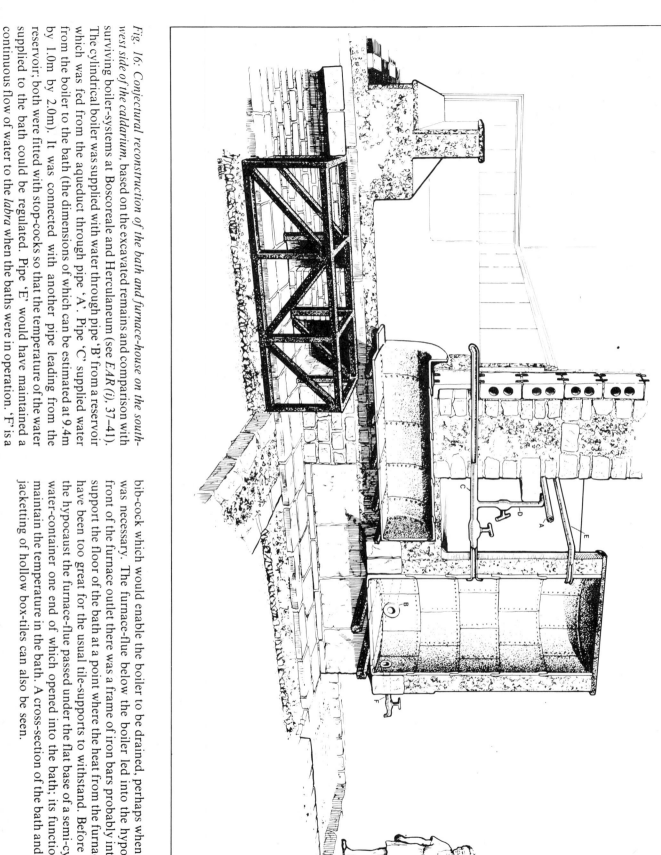

Fig. 16: Conjectural reconstruction of the bath and furnace-house on the south-west side of the caldarium, based on the excavated remains and comparison with surviving boiler-systems at Boscoreale and Herculaneum (see EAR (i), 37–41).
The cylindrical boiler was supplied with water through pipe 'A'. Pipe 'C' supplied water which was fed from the aqueduct through pipe 'B' from a reservoir from the boiler to the bath (the dimensions of which can be estimated at 9.4m by 1.0m by 2.0m). It was connected with another pipe leading from the reservoir; both were fitted with stop-cocks so that the temperature of the water supplied to the bath could be regulated. Pipe 'E' would have maintained a continuous flow of water to the *labra* when the baths were in operation. 'F' is a

bib-cock which would enable the boiler to be drained, perhaps when cleaning was necessary. The furnace-flue below the boiler led into the hypocaust; in front of the furnace outlet there was a frame of iron bars probably intended to support the floor of the bath at a point where the heat from the furnace would have been too great for the usual tile-supports to withstand. Before reaching the hypocaust the furnace-flue passed under the flat base of a semi-cylindrical water-container one end of which opened into the bath; its function was to maintain the temperature in the bath. A cross-section of the bath and the wall-jacketting of hollow box-tiles can also be seen.

Fig. 17: Model of legionary baths. Service area and exterior of *caldarium* looking north.

and Caerleon (erected *c.* 80).[39] All four of these buildings have axially-symmetrical plans which probably derive from as yet unrecognised prototypes.

In spite of the cramped nature of the accommodation in the fortress at Exeter (p. 20), the baths show that some attempt was made to provide facilities for the legionaries when they were off-duty.[40] No doubt hygiene played some part in the cultivation of military *disciplina,* but the size and architectural sophistication of legionary bath-houses suggests that the promotion of hygiene was only one of their functions. They can be seen as the counterparts of the public baths to be found in any Roman town where the inhabitants bathed at their leisure and amused themselves with ball-games, gambling and gossip.

The *fabrica (Figs. 19, 20)*

The *fabrica* occupied a site in the angle between the *via principalis* and the north-west stretch of the *via sagularis.* Its construction took place some years after the foundation of the fortress, and its site was at first occupied by two or more buildings associated with four pits, the fillings of which contained much charcoal and burnt clay. Only the eastern corner of the *fabrica* was excavated (Fig. 19); the rest of the site has now been obliterated by modern development. The principal feature was an aisled hall 9m wide with at least four bays and a room measuring 9m by 7.5m at its south-east end. Its construction was substantial: the post-trenches were 90cm in depth and the posts themselves had been driven into the ground a further 40cm. This suggests that the hall rose to a considerable height, and that its nave may have been lit by a clerestory.[41] The corner of another room was excavated adjacent to the street which led to the *via principalis;* it was separated from the range containing the aisled hall by an entry *c.* 6m in width. The entry may have been intended for the use of pedestrians and was probably covered, because it had a clay floor which was not metalled, although very worn. In the room at the south-east end of the hall the floor was covered with trampled occupation-debris, but no evidence for metal-working was found. On three sides of the room at a distance of about a metre from the walls a narrow slot was found, possibly the bedding-trench for the supports of racks or work-benches.

The levels inside the aisled hall had been cut through by many later features but extensive traces of some of the activities which had taken place there still survived. Most prominent were a large number of shallow troughs no more than 20cm in depth and 40–50cm in width, although their lengths varied

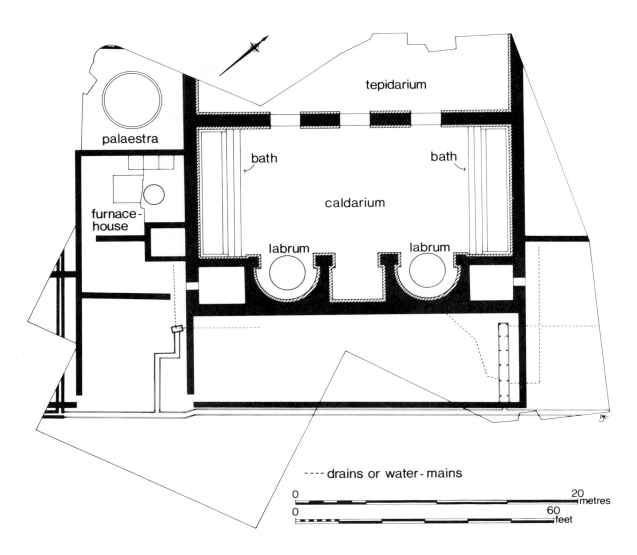

Fig. 18: Reconstruction of the ground-plan of the excavated portion of the legionary baths.

between 50cm and 4m. Their sides were lined with stakes clearly intended to hold plank linings in position. Emplacements of similar type have been noted at Verulamium; they were filled with 'fine sandy earth interleaved with much bronze powder and tiny lumps of this metal' and also some iron powder, and were interpreted as 'an apparatus for trapping the waste from lathe-turning, engraving or filing bronzes, with the intention of re-smelting it later'.[42] One trough (701, see Fig. 19) in the *fabrica* at Exeter contained similar material, but the others were filled with charcoal and bronze scraps, presumably debris from the floor of the hall deposited after the plank-linings had been removed and the troughs went out of use.

The arrangement of the troughs and other features in the hall was orderly and can be described according to the bays in which they were situated, starting from the south-east (the numbers in brackets refer to features shown on Fig. 19):

Bay 1 was partly screened off from the rest of the hall by a partition between the aisle posts (979, 981, 1215). Its floor was covered with charcoal and burnt clay on top of which was a hearth (810).

Bay 2 contained wooden troughs on its south-east and north-west sides (1003 and 1176); these were replaced by a second set of troughs (1004 and 805). Subsequently, the troughs were filled with charcoal and debris from bronze-working; the latest activities in this area were represented by two hearths and a number of features including shallow rounded scoops (e.g. 1235 and 1237) which could have been settings for amphora-bases re-used as water-containers.[43]

Bays 3 and 4 in the earliest phase were occupied by a long plank-lined feature (985) which probably served as a drain. This was superseded by another probable drain on the south-west side of the aisle

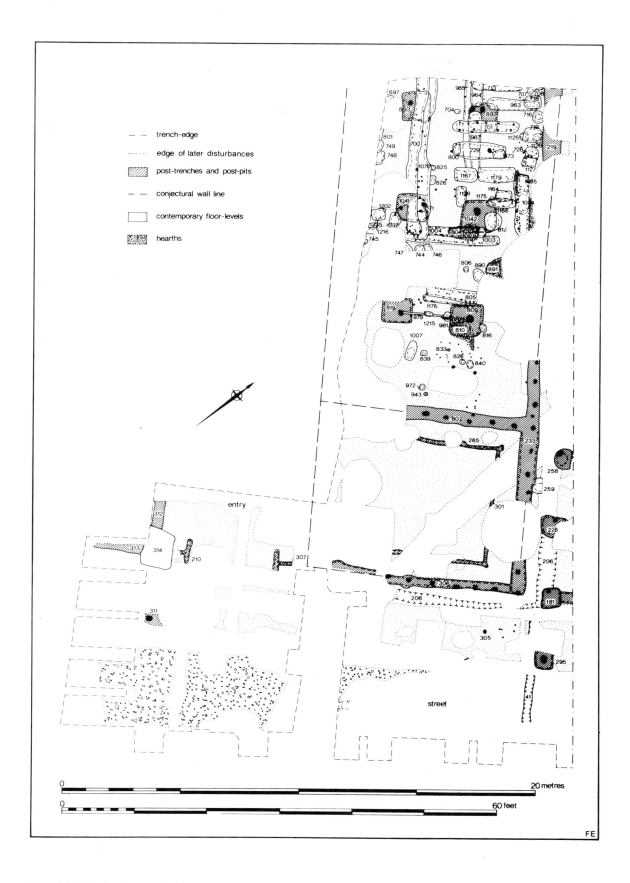

Fig. 19: The legionary *fabrica* (workshop); on upper right-hand side, the aisled hall with successive hearths, drains and rectangular emplacements.

Fig. 20: The aisled hall of the *fabrica* looking south-east. This photograph serves to illustrate the damage which most Roman structures at Exeter have sustained from medieval and later activities; the bases of a number of circular or rectangular medieval pits can be seen. In the upper part of the photograph parts of two circular trenches can be seen; these may represent prehistoric hut-circles (p. 16). 2m scale.

(1070, later replaced by 700). The first drain (985) was cut by two troughs (984 and 987) which were probably contemporary with a third to the north-east (963); these contained iron slag and fragments of bronze. A later series of troughs contained debris only from bronze-working. Shallow scoops, possibly the settings for amphora-bases (see above), were also found.

The bronze objects from the troughs and from the layers of debris on the floor of the hall provide some information about the manufacturing processes in the *fabrica*. The majority are off-cuts: thin bronze sheets, short lengths and coils of wire, and three bars, the ends of which appear to have been struck off with a chisel. Nails and tacks with flat or domed heads, some apparently unused and others with bent shanks, were also found, as well as fragments of two tweezers. The only certainly identifiable objects which appear to be unfinished or defective are three pins; their shanks are roughly square in section and their heads mis-shapen (Fig. 25, 9–11). Three objects, flat plates with thin shanks, are probably rough-outs, possibly of girdle-plate tie-hooks for *loricae segmentatae* (see below; Fig. 25, 12–14). There were also two complete examples of this type of fitting and three hinge-plates; they had been used and preserved traces of the rivets which secured them to the iron plates of the *lorica*.

The armour worn by legionaries at this period (*lorica segementata*), consisting of iron plates secured to leather straps and fastened together with small buckles and tie-hooks, would have required frequent repairs to its flimsy fittings. There are a number of half-finished articles from forts and fortresses which provide evidence for the manufacture of these fittings (perhaps also of complete *loricae segmentatae*) and of belt-plates, belt-buckles and other fasteners.[44] Evidence for the manufacture of less utilitarian types of armour comes from Haltern, where a fragment of an unfinished iron masked helmet was found, and from the site at Kingsholm near Gloucester (p. 12) which produced a decorative bronze plate; the latter was intended to cover the cheek-piece of an iron helmet, but clearly had never been fitted into place.[45]

Production in the *fabricae* was not confined to items of armour: half-finished brooches have been found at Vindonissa in Switzerland and at Rheingönheim and probably Risstissen in Germany.[46]

Barrack-blocks *(Figs. 7, 21)*

Parts of four barrack-blocks have been excavated in the northern corner of the fortress (Fig. 7). Two adjacent to the *fabrica* faced each other across a street 5m in width and formed a pair. A post-trench belonging to an earlier building was found on their site, and shallow pits were found under the street which separated the barracks. Similar features were encountered on the site of the *fabrica* (p. 31); this suggests that both the *fabrica* and the adjacent pair of barracks were erected some years after the foundation of the fortress. On two occasions both barracks were rebuilt to the same plan. The other two barracks to the north-east were built back-to-back and belonged to two adjoining pairs (Fig. 21); the existence of another pair of barrack-blocks to the north-east, completing a cohort-block, seems very probable. No traces of previous buildings were found on their site. The barracks had been rebuilt to roughly the same plan on two occasions, as in the case of those adjacent to the *fabrica*. The technique employed in the construction of the four barracks was the same in all three phases: post-trenches up to *c.* 70cm in depth marked the position of timber uprights which would have supported walls of wattle and daub. An unusual feature, at least in legionary (although not auxiliary) accommodation,[47] is the absence of post-trenches dividing the *contubernia* of the two barracks to the north-east in their final phase of construction; they were presumably separated by partitions which were supported by sill-beams laid at floor-level.

Although parts of the two barracks to the north-east lay outside the excavated areas, it is still possible to reconstruct their overall dimensions. The centurions' quarters, which lay next to the *via sagularis,* were *c.* 19.5m in length; the overall length of the block of *contubernia* was *c.*42.5m. In the second phase the inner rooms of the *contubernia* each measured *c.* 3–3.5m sq., giving an area of *c.* 9–11 sq. m, which is smaller than the 18 sq. m usually allowed for *contubernia* in first-century legionary barrack-blocks (Table 1) and closer to the 10 Roman ft. sq. prescribed for the area of a *papilio* or tent in a temporary camp.[48] The Exeter barrack-blocks are thus appreciably smaller than other legionary examples, which from Augustan times are generally between 70m and 80m in length, and sometimes rather larger (Table 1). V.A. Maxfield noted that the centurions' quarters in the Exeter barracks were of normal size, and that the reduction in length was achieved by allowing a much smaller area than usual for the *contubernia*.[49] The same is true of the barracks at Haltern (Table 1).

The barracks next to the *fabrica* are distinguished from those to the north-east by the presence of two rectangular buildings at their south-east ends; in their first and second phases of construction these buildings were probably free-standing (although they were apparently erected at the same time

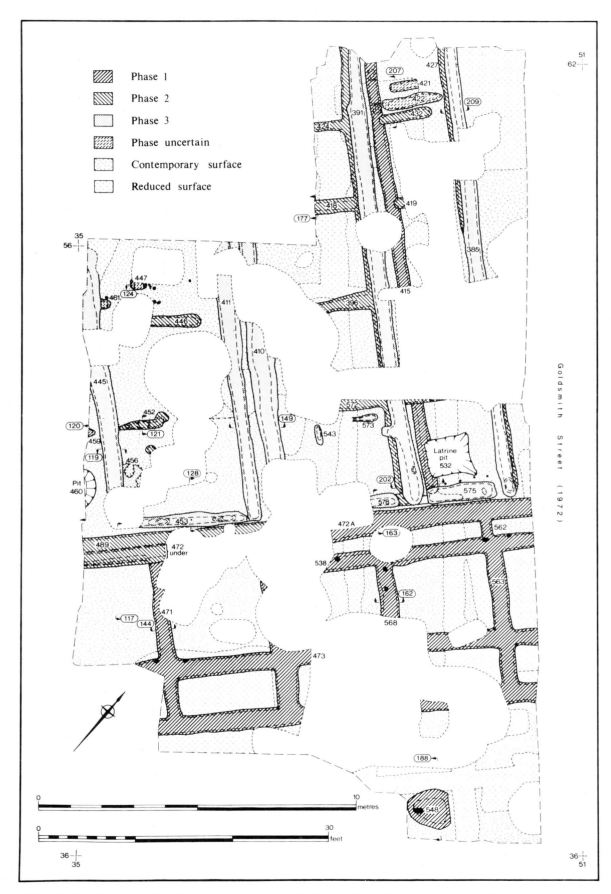

Fig. 21: South-east ends of two legionary barrack-blocks (showing three phases of construction) and part of a possible store-building on the south-east side.

Fortress.	Date of foundation.	Size (ha).	Approx. length of barracks (m).	Number of *contubernia*.	Approx. size of sleeping-quarters (sq.m).	Approx. length of centurions' quarters (m).	References.
Dangstetten	Augustan	17.0+	80	?	?	?	Fingerlin 1971, 209–10, Beil. 28.
Haltern	Augustan	16.7	70	10–12	?	24	Von Schnurbein 1974, 68–9.
Colchester	*c.* 43	19.4	79	?	?	22	Crummy 1977, 69–74, Figs. 3 and 4.
Exeter	*c.* 55–60	15.4	62	14	9–11.5	19.5	-
Gloucester	*c.* 69	17.5	72?	12–13?	20	19	Hurst 1972, 39, Fig. 2; 1974, Fig. 4.
Caerleon	*c.* 75	20.5	74	12	17	22	Boon 1972, 85–9.
Inchtuthil	*c.* 83	20.0	82	14	18.5	22	Richmond 1959 Abb. 18.

Table 1: dimensions of timber barrack-blocks (excluding those of the first cohort) in first-century legionary fortresses. N.B. the dimensions of the stone barrack-blocks are given in the case of Caerleon, but these were probably the same size as their predecessors which had timber superstructures above stone footings (Boon 1972, 25–6).

as the barracks), but in the third phase their north-west walls formed the end walls of the adjoining *contubernia*. The rectangular buildings resemble centurions' quarters, although they appear to be shorter (17.4m by 13m and 17.7m by *c.* 10.5m in the last phase of construction) than those belonging to the barracks to the north-east and are not sited next to the *via sagularis*, as was customary. These barracks, which were apparently built some years after the foundation of the fortress (p. 35), have been claimed as possible accommodation for *immunes*, soldiers exempt from ordinary garrison duties because they had special skills.[50] However, D. Baatz has shown that there is no firm evidence that *immunes* were provided with accommodation separate from that of other legionaries.[51] He suggests that barracks of this type, which did not form part of a cohort-block, served as accommodation for 'special' groups and were occupied by vexillations of veterans, civilians in charge of the baggage-train or auxiliaries, all groups which did not belong to the ten cohorts of the legion.[52]

Granaries *(Fig. 7)*

Traces of one or more granaries covering an area of at least 40m by 15m have been recovered from a site between the *via praetoria* and the street on the south-east side of the *fabrica*. The granaries had been supported on a grid of pile-driven posts, which were represented by a series of post-holes *c.* 30cm in depth. Two or more phases of construction could be deduced. Granaries of similar type and date have been found in the fortress at Usk and outside the fort at Valkenburg in Holland.[53]

Other buildings in the *praetentura* *(Figs. 7, 21)*

A street and parts of at least three buildings have been excavated in the area between the cohort-block in the northern corner of the fortress and the *via praetoria*. The street, which was *c.* 4.5m wide, was found at a distance of *c.* 64.5m from the *via praetoria*; it continued for a distance of no more than 15m to the south-west, although in the early town it was extended to join the street on the south-east side of the *fabrica* (i.e. between *Insulae* IV and IX, see Fig. 27 and p. 47). Post-trenches belonging to two separate buildings were found on the south-east side of this street. Another building was found further to the south-west, next to the cohort-block; it consisted of at least five pairs of rooms (Fig. 21). The larger rooms measured up to 3.4m by 3m, and the smaller rooms 3m by 1.2m; three of the larger rooms, however, appear to have been reduced in size during the course of their construction, leaving a narrow space between their rear walls and the ends of the adjacent barrack-blocks. These rooms resemble *contubernia,* but the restoration of the building as a barrack-block presents considerable problems. Its length would have been in excess of 65m if it extended as far as the north-east stretch of the *via sagularis,* compared with the length of *c.* 62m established for the barracks in the adjoining cohort-block. Furthermore, there is not enough space for another barrack-block on the north-west side of the street referred to above. Thus, unless the block of rooms formed part of an isolated barrack-block similar to those adjacent to the *fabrica,* which appeared to provide accommodation for special groups (p. 37), another interpretation of their function must be found. In the supply-base at Richborough there is a partly excavated building dated to *c.* 50–60, which consists of three ranges surrounding a courtyard.[54] The southern range has eight pairs of rooms similar in size to those at Exeter (*c.* 3.75m sq. and 3.75m by 1.5m), the smaller rooms facing onto the courtyard. Along the inner side of the western range ran a veranda, which appeared to have continued along the southern side of the courtyard. The building was identified as an 'administrative block' or a *mansio,* but was perhaps more likely to have been a store-house of courtyard-type.[55] The block of rooms at Exeter may have belonged to a similar building.

Buildings in the *latera praetorii* (Fig. 7)

In 1945–6 two timber buildings and a length of street were excavated on a site on the south-west side of the *via principalis.*[56] They were sealed beneath the gravel metalling of the market-place on the south-west side of the *forum* and therefore can be dated to before *c.* 80 (p. 52). The street was 3m in width with a drain which was once perhaps covered with planking running down its centre. Only one wall of the building on the north-west side of the street was traced. The building on the opposite side of the street consisted of a room measuring *c.* 11.1m by 7.75m, with another room to the south-west and possibly a veranda on the south-east side. The large room had a clay floor with a hearth made of tiles set in its centre; the floor of the adjoining room, also of clay, was covered with patches of burning and refuse including crucibles. The construction-technique of the building is of interest. The walls consisted of timber uprights embedded to a depth of *c.* 60cm and regularly spaced at intervals of about a metre; in section the timbers were mostly round with a diameter of *c.* 20cm, although a few were square. The bases of the timbers were probably placed in post-trenches; these were not traced, but in dry weather conditions they can be extremely difficult to detect. Between the posts narrow slots *c.* 3.5cm in width and *c.*7–14cm in depth were found; these were interpreted as bedding slots either for the uprights of wattles or for thin timber sills in which the uprights were inserted.

Finds from the occupation-layers were pre-Flavian in date, and it would seem in consequence that the buildings belonged to the fortress; this is confirmed by the apparent absence of earlier buildings on their site. The street which ran between these buildings may represent one of the thoroughfares flanking the *principia;* these are usually of a considerable width, as at Caerleon and at Lambaesis in North Africa, but occasionally are little more than alley-ways, as at Nijmegen.[57] The building on the north-west side of the street would then represent part of the *principia,* the dimensions of which can be calculated at *c.* 54.5m from north-west to south-east and at least 64.5m from north-east to south-west.[58] The building on the south-east side of the street is likely to have formed part of the barracks of the first cohort, which would have had a length in excess of 64.5m; the width of the plot they occupied would have been *c.* 129m.[59]

In 1972 on the site of the barrack-blocks next to the *fabrica* (p. 35) the sculptured torso of a bird was found in the filling of a late first-century pit (p. 53; Fig. 22).[60] It is the only known example in Purbeck marble of figure-sculpture in the round. The torso, which appears to be roughly life-size, is probably that of an eagle, and may have formed an adjunct of a sculpture of Jupiter, or of an emperor in Jupiter's guise, the most likely setting for which would have been the *principia.*

Part of a building north-west of the *principia* was excavated in 1973. Its post-trenches were up to 1.2m in depth, and the building seemed to have been constructed on the same substantial scale as the *fabrica* (p. 31). The ends of the posts had survived and were of oak. Not enough is known of the building to determine its function, but its position within the fortress and the probable proportions of its plot correspond to those of a building at Caerleon which has been claimed as a stable.[61]

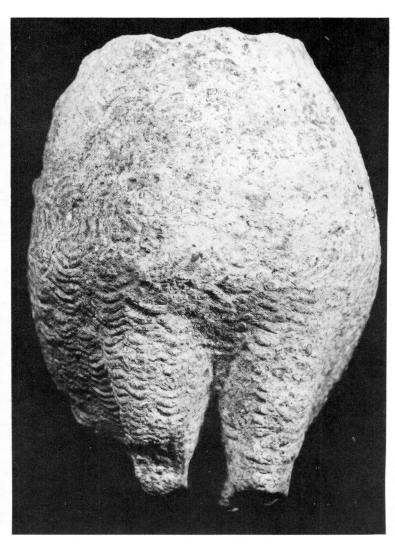

Fig. 22: Sculptured torso of a bird, probably that of an eagle, in Purbeck marble. It may have formed part of a sculptered representation of the emperor in the guise of Jupiter which would have been accommodated in the headquarters building. Height 204mm.

In 1974 post-trenches belonging to three successive timber buildings were observed in contractors' trenches at Mary Arches Street; it was not possible to determine the plan of the buildings.

Retentura *(Fig. 7)*
Nothing certain is known of the fortress lay-out in this area, but the fragmentary plans of timber buildings of military date have come to light at Mermaid Yard,[62] and finds of early material have been made on the site of the Western (or Lower) Market from 1835 onwards and on a site near Fore St in 1952.[63]

The dating evidence
The evidence for the dates of both the foundation and demolition of the fortress has been discussed in detail elsewhere.[64] The general character of early coins and pottery from all contexts at Exeter points to a foundation-date after *c.* 55. A survey by B.M. Dickinson of first-century potters' stamps on samian ware from excavations (up to November 1978) and collections in the Rougemont House Museum, notably that made by Shortt (p. 2), has amplified this evidence (Fig. 23). The dates of some of the stamps are earlier than those of the decorated samian vessels;[65] nevertheless, none of the earliest stamps belongs to the potters who ceased work before *c.* 55. Two finds from early fortress levels are also of importance:
(i) a samian stamp of *c.* 55–70 was recovered from the base of the rampart in Mermaid Yard. Some doubt must attach to the provenance of this piece because it was not possible to determine whether the rampart had been repaired at this point.

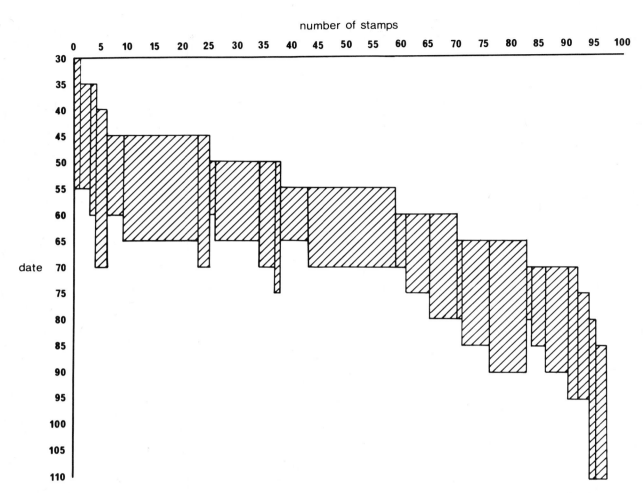

Fig. 23: Histogram of first-century samian stamps from Exeter; compiled from information supplied by B.M. Dickinson.

(ii) a group of twelve samian vessels with a *terminus post quem* of *c.* 60 came from the filling of the smaller, innermost legionary ditch. This displayed few signs of weathering and none of recutting; it was probably filled in shortly after the foundation of the fortress (p. 23).

This provides further support for a foundation-date of *c.* 55–60, which, in the absence of monumental inscriptions, is difficult to define more closely.

Dating evidence from the final phase of construction of the barracks which formed part of the cohort-block in the northern corner of the fortress makes it certain that they were erected after *c.* 70. One post-trench contained a coin of Nero (*RIC* 286) which had been well-circulated, and another a group of six samian vessels: three plain pre-Flavian forms, another of Neronian-Vespasianic date, and a Dr. 29 and a Dr. 30, both dating from *c.* 70. A group of samian from the floor of the *fabrica* was closed by a Dr. 29 dated to *c.* 70–85.

The dating evidence for the abandonment of the fortress and the possible works-depot or supply-base has been summarised elsewhere and need not be repeated; it accords well with a date of *c.* 75.[66]

Industries and supplies *(Fig. 24)*

Traces of contemporary industrial activities have been found in the vicinity of the fortress. At Southernhay West a deposit of clay containing many tile-wasters was found below the later Roman town rampart and above a layer containing pre-Flavian material. Tile-wasters were also incorporated within the body of the rampart 28m further north and in the make-up levels of the road leading to the *porta praetoria* of the fortress.[67] These observations suggest that the tile-kilns serving the fortress were located outside the eastern corner of the defences in the same area as the *canabae* (p. 41). Tiles were employed principally in the construction of the legionary baths, but also elsewhere within the fortress.

Pottery-kilns may also have been located in the vicinity of these tile-kilns. A class of pottery found in the fortress and early civil levels includes a fabric which looks very like the locally-produced tiles.[68] This industry was not of great importance; in large groups it represents only between 6.5% and 13.5% of the total assemblage, but nevertheless its products have been recognised in the forts at Okehampton and Nanstallon, and in a native settlement at Carvossa, near Probus in Cornwall.[69] Traces of a kiln producing flagons and mortaria stamped with the name (?) VITANI or VITANII were found outside the south-western defences of the fortress (Fig. 25, 3); no mortaria bearing this stamps have been recovered from within the fortress and it is uncertain whether this industry was long-lived. Local production of *terra nigra* vessels, small cups and platters in fine grey or black fabric, is also possible.[70]

The majority of the coarse wares used by the legion were produced by the black-burnished ware industry of south-east Dorset, although several minor industries, the precise locations of which are unknown, also supplied appreciable amounts.[71] A few vessels in a gabbroic fabric have been recovered from fortress levels and were produced in the Lizard peninsula in Cornwall. Pottery imported from the continent, although mostly confined to fine wares, samian, amphorae and some types of mortaria, makes up from between 30% and 43.5% of the larger contemporary assemblages. Types to be found on any large military site in southern Britain during the third quarter of the first century are represented: samian from south Gaul and (although rarely) Lezoux, fine wares from Lyon, Spain and central Gaul; *terra nigra* and mortaria from northern Gaul; and amphorae from Spain and southern Gaul. The only unusual feature about these imports is the presence of no fewer than ten Spanish colour-coated vessels, for only 19 vessels are recorded from other sites in Britain; the relatively large number from Exeter may perhaps be explained by the fact that Exeter (or Topsham, p. 44) would have been the first port of call for ships bound from Spain to Britain.[72] Many other commodities must have been imported, particularly foodstuffs, but with the exception of glass no traces of these have survived. The only other materials which can be easily traced to their places of origin are types of building-stone used in the construction of the legionary baths.[73] Considerable quantities of Purbeck marble from south-east Dorset were employed for internal decorative features. Trap, the stone employed for the construction of walls and also for the metalling of streets within the fortress, was probably quarried from Rougemont, just beyond the northern corner of the defences; Triassic sandstone, which was used for architectural details, was obtained from a quarry in east Devon, possibly along the coast between Budleigh Salterton and Sidmouth. White Lias for floor-quarries was perhaps derived from a source near Langport in Somerset or in the vicinity of Axminster; grey mudstone was quarried locally for the same purpose.

Contemporary sites in the neighbourhood of the fortress *(Fig. 24)*
i) The possible works-depot or supply-base:
Excavations on sites to the south-east of the Coombe valley have recovered extensive remains of timber buildings of military type.[74] The two principal sites are separated by the line of the road from Topsham. The buildings south-west of the line showed three major phases of construction, those to the north-east only one. Since the latter were built over two cremations dating to *c.* 65 (see below), they would appear to represent an enlargement of the original establishment. The precise function of these buildings is uncertain, but they may well represent a works-depot or supply-base.

In 1964 a substantial ditch was found below the rampart of the Roman town next to the South Gate, running at right angles to these later defences.[75] The function of the ditch is uncertain, but it may mark the position of an enclosure on the south-west side of the road from Topsham.

ii) The canabae: the most likely position for the *canabae* is on the level ground beyond the *porta praetoria* of the fortress. Post-war excavations produced some evidence of early occupation south-east of the road leading to the gate[76] and work in Southernhay Gardens (1974) has located two small timber buildings and a well of first-century date.[77]

iii) Cemeteries:
The two cremations referred to above probably belonged to a cemetery alongside the road leading to the *porta principalis dextra*. Although partly removed by later pits the cremations still contained a rich collection of objects, including a bronze lamp and a statuette of Victory (Fig. 25, 5, 8). The wealth of the grave-goods and proximity to the *porta principalis dextra* suggest that this cemetery was dedicated to legionary rather than civilian use.[78]

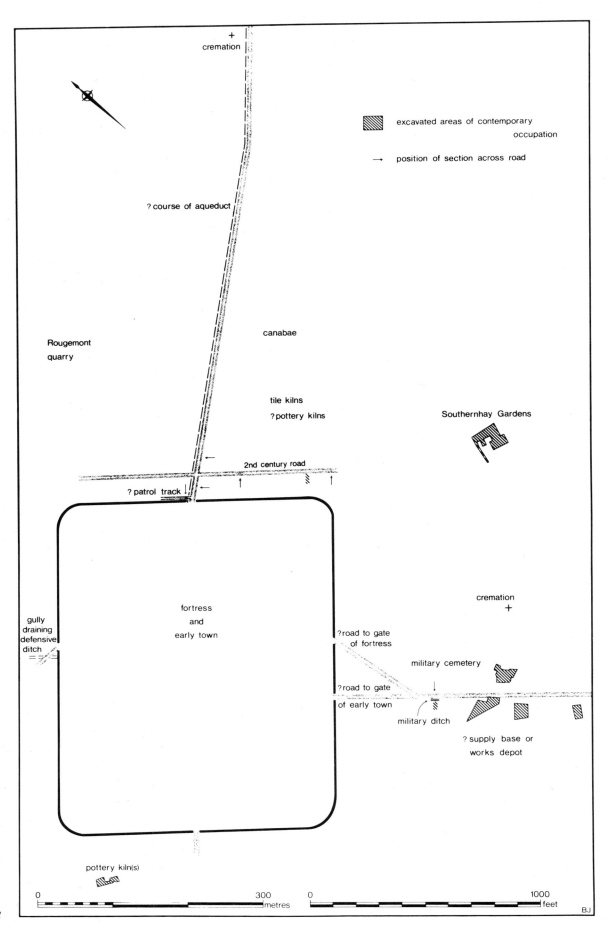

Fig. 24

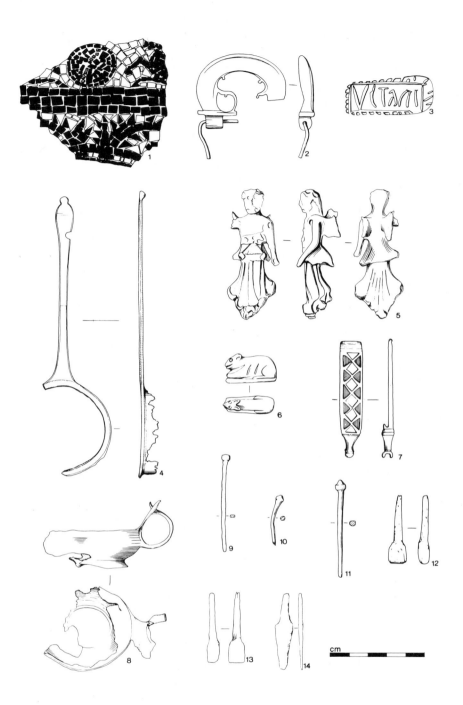

Fig. 25: Finds from the period of the legionary fortress. (1) Drawing of mosaic fragment from legionary baths (p. 28) showing two confronted hoofed animals with a circular motif between them (the cross-hatched *tesserae* are samian ware); below a plain band there are plant-fronds (*EAR (i)*, 132–4, Pl. XVIA). (2) Military belt-buckle in bone of a type more commonly made in bronze; from context dating to *c.* 75. (3) Mortarium stamp of VITANUS or VITANIUS from kilns operating in the late Neronian or early Flavian period outside the south-west defences of the fortress (p. 41). (4) Bronze ladle from a pit probably falling within the limits of the *fabrica*-site (*EAR (i)*, 7). (5) Bronze figurine of Victory (?) from a cremation dating to *c.* 55–65 (p. 41). (6) Bronze model of a mouse from a pit near the southern corner of the fortress. (7) Strap-end with enamelled decoration in red and green; from a late first-century pit cut through the corner of the barrack-block adjacent to the *fabrica*. (8) Bronze lamp (nozzle broken off) from the same cremation as no. 5. (9–11) Mis-shapen and possibly unfinished bronze pins from the *fabrica* (p. 35). (12–14) Bronze rough -outs, possibly for tie-hooks of *loricae segmentatae,* from the *fabrica* (p. 35). Scale: no. 1, 1 : 4; nos. 2–14, 1 : 2.

Fig. 24: The surroundings of the fortress and early town. Arrows show the position of sections across roads.

Pre-Flavian material, including another bronze lamp, from the parish of St David's probably points to the site of another early cemetery, some 0.5km. (400 yards) north of the fortress.[79]

iv) The Stoke Hill 'signal-station':

In 1953 a double-ditched enclosure was discovered on the highest point of Stoke Hill (*c.* 158m O.D.) some 2.5km (1.5 miles) due north of the fortress. The outer, subannular enclosure was roughly 110m across and the inner enclosure was *c.* 33.5m square with an entrance on the east side. Excavation proved that banks or ramparts were associated with both these ditches.[80] No buildings were found in either enclosure, and the only datable finds were a coin of Carausius and a Dr.38 imitation (possibly Oxford Ware), which were not in contexts associated with the primary occupation of the site. The enclosures were at first thought to represent a late-Roman signal-station, but then comparison with Martinhoe and Old Burrow led to the suggestion of a first-century date.[81] Another possibility is that the site is pre-Roman; double-ditched enclosures are a common settlement type in and around the Exe Valley, and although their date has not yet been established by excavation, the type is likely to originate in the early Iron Age (p. 16). The absence of first-century finds from the site, a considerable area of which has been explored, favours this interpretation.

v) Topsham:

Scattered finds of first-century material at Topsham, some 6.5km (3.8 miles) from Exeter at the head of the Exe estuary, have been found over an area of 25ha (60 acres) to the north of the modern town. A 'farmstead' occupied from *c.* 50/55 to 70/75 was recently excavated in the vicinity.[82] C.A. Ralegh Radford has suggested, with due circumspection, that the traces of early occupation are to be associated with a port or naval base, a view that has gained acceptance.[83] V.A. Maxfield has rightly stressed that this interpretation is supported only by the mere fact of first-century occupation.[84] Although the Exe is now tidal to a distance of only 3.5km (1.8 miles) above Topsham, where the river has been blocked since the thirteenth century, it was very probably navigable as far as Exeter in Roman times.

NOTES

1. K. Jackson in Rivet 1970, 75, casting doubt on earlier views which derived *Isca* from the Celtic *Eisca,* meaning 'a river abounding in fish (I. Williams in Fox 1952, 5–6); Rivet and Smith 1979, 376–8.
2. Rivet 1974, 61.
3. Camden (Gough 1806, 35–6) was the first to doubt that the legion was stationed at Exeter. The first writer in recent times to argue the contrary case for legionary occupation was R.G. Goodchild (unpublished thesis, 1939, 56–7); he accepted Ptolemy's ascription which he considered to be supported by the large amounts of mid first-century material from Exeter; he also identified a legionary scabbard-chape amongst finds from the excavation of a masonry building on *Insula* XXXIV, site 1 (Fig. 37; Montague and Morris 1933–6 Fig. 2, 1).
4. Birley 1953, 34–5; Rivet 1974, 61.
5. Ptolemy placed *Isca*-Exeter only 115 Roman miles from London, instead of the true figure of 170, and made it adjoin the wrong river, the Alaunus (probably the Devon Axe) instead of the Isca (Exe). A.L.F. Rivet (1974, 72) has suggested that Ptolemy's list of contemporary legionary dispositions may also have included the locations of the fortresses, and that the shorter distance of *Isca*-Caerleon from London (133 Roman miles) may have led him to alter the position of *Isca*-Exeter accordingly.
6. Rivet 1970, 60 (*Iter* v).
7. Stevens 1927, Pl. facing p. 189.
8. Richmond and Crawford 1949, 17.
9. *RIB*(i), 1843, 1844.
10. J. E. Bogaers in *J. Roman Stud.,* 57 (1967) 233.
11. A drawing by W. Schellinks (1662) shows the medieval Exe bridge with pack-horses fording the river alongside it, perhaps so as to avoid paying tolls (reproduced in Hoskins 1960, Pl.III facing p. 17).
12. Hoskins 1960, 3.
13. The contours on Fig. 5 are those of the modern city, and have been much altered since the early Roman period by quarrying and the partial infilling of valleys. Excavations in Coombe St (1979) demonstrated that material was dumped in the Coombe valley in late Roman times. Much of Rougemont is likely to have been removed by quarrying throughout the Roman period, and its top

may have been levelled when the Norman castle was erected. The Longbrook and Shutebrook valleys were partly filled during the course of the nineteenth century.
14. *EAR* (i), 6.
15. Von Petrikovits 1975, 113. The reader is directed to the collection of fortress-plans in this work to avoid the repetition of references.
16. ibid., 114.
17. *EAR* (i), 8.
18. Vexillation fortresses (p. 13), which at 8–12ha (20–30 acres) in area are markedly smaller than the fortresses listed here, are excluded from consideration. They were probably garrisoned by both auxiliaries and legionaires (Frere and St Joseph 1974, 6–7). The only examples where some estimate of the size of the garrison can be attempted is Longthorpe, which had an area of 10.9ha (27.3 acres); it was argued that there was room for 1440 or 1760 legionaries and *c.* 960–1000 auxiliaries (ibid., 34–5).
19. Because of their small size it has been suggested that Lincoln and Gloucester were not garrisoned by full legions (Lincoln: Petch 1962, 48; Gloucester: Manning 1976, 35–6).
20. Von Schnurbein 1974, 46; review of *idem* in *Britannia,* 8 (1977) 463–6.
21. See Table 1 and von Petrikovits 1975, Bilder 2, 13.
22. Bogaers and Haalebos 1977, 104–5.
23. Von Petrikovits 1975, 116.
24. Von Petrikovits' (1975, 116) calculations exclude the space occupied by the streets within the fortresses.
25. As at Inchtuthil, Caerleon, Carnuntum and Lauriacum.
26. The small size of the fortress may have been necessary because of the topography of the site (see p. 16).
27. The erroneous ascription of the legion to Exeter in the mid second century by Ptolemy may also be relevant (p. 16).
28. Bidwell and Boon 1976.
29. The outer ditch did not cut the inner, as was incorrectly stated in *EAR* (i). 3; a third ditch dating to the civil period (p. 47) had not been recognised at the time and its base, which cut the inner ditch, was thought to form part of the outer ditch.
30. Manning 1978, 71 (fig.), 73 (fig.).
31. Crummy 1977, 70.

32. Frere and St. Joseph 1974, 10.

33. In terms of the later town plan, *Insula* XXI, site 1 (Fig. 37).

34. The metalling may even be associated with a parade-ground on the level ground below Rougemont.

35. Morris 1933–6, 228–31, PL. LIV; not noted in the description of the fortress in *EAR* (i).

36. Fox 1966, 49, Fig. 9.

37. Excavation report in *EAR* (i), 22–66. For a comparison of their size see ibid., Table 5 and von Petrikovits 1975, Bild 28.

38. *EAR* (i), 134.

39. See further, *EAR* (i), 43–50. Recent excavations by D. Zienkiewicz (*Britannia,* 10 (1979) 273–4, at Caerleon have shown that the plan of the *frigidarium* is similar in some respects to that of the *caldarium* at Vindonissa.

40. The earliest legionary baths of a substantial size and of orthodox design are in the fortress at Vindonissa (Laur-Belart 1935, 46–56); they can be dated to the reign of Claudius (Fellman 1958, 40). However, three successive buildings on a site to the north of the *principia* in the Tiberian fortress at Vindonissa represent bath-houses of a most unusual type. The first of these was a circular room *c.* 7.8m in diameter; its function is uncertain, but a granite *labrum* was found on its floor and may demonstrate that the room was associated with a bath-house. In the late 20s a block of three rooms measuring *c.* 33.75m by 22.5m overall was erected on the site; they had clay walls supported by timber uprights, and the floors were also of clay. One of the rooms, which probably served as a *caldarium,* contained a lead-lined bath; outside the building, immediately adjacent to the bath, a furnace was found where water could have been heated. The other two rooms perhaps served as an *apodyterium* (changing-room) and a *tepidarium.* This building was replaced by another of similar extent and plan but with stone walls in *c.* 30. None of these buildings was equipped with hypocausts, and presumably the *caldaria* and *tepidaria* were heated by braziers. *Piscinae* (pools) were found outside these two later buildings. The excavation of these buildings is described in Laur-Belart 1933 and Simonett 1934, 1936.

41. The *fabrica* in the *intervallum* at Regensburg, a hall which measured 60m by 9m, was at least 7m in height (von Petrikovits 1975, 89).

42. Frere 1972, 18–9, where reference is made to other examples, as yet unpublished, from Catterick. It is doubtful whether the material in the troughs at Exeter represents the waste from lathe-turning, a technique most commonly employed in the production of metal vessels, because no swarf, which is the most characteristic by-product of the process, was found. At both Exeter and Verulamium the material in the troughs was fine and densely stratified, as if deposited by water. It may have resulted from the use of grindstones to put the finishing-touches to small objects; water would have been used as a lubricant. However, the contents of the emplacements at Catterick yielded 'characteristic curled shavings of corroded metal, as though they had been derived from lathe-turned pieces' (J.S. Wacher in *Britannia,* 4 (1973) 351).

43. They resembled the settings for amphora-bases re-used as urinals in the service-area of the legionary baths (*EAR* (i), 37, 64).

44. References collected in von Petrikovits 1974, 6n.9 and Oldenstein 1976, 71–3. An unfinished fastener similar to examples from Hod Hill (Brailsford 1962, A.97,98) was found at Mainz (Behrens 1917–18, 29, Abb. 9.1), and an unfinished buckle of late Roman type has been found at Bonn (von Petrikovits 1974, 6n.9). The most extensive collection of unfinished objects was recovered in the area of the *fabrica* at the Roman fort of Rheingönheim: in addition to off-cuts similar to those from Exeter there were two fleur-de-lys buckle-tongues, two fasteners resembling the example from Mainz mentioned above, three studs with petal decoration, two crest-holders and what appears to be a belt-plate (Ulbert 1969a, Taf. 26.18,19; Taf. 26.23,24; Taf. 29.5–7; Taf. 30.10,11; Taf. 27.6)

45. Kropatschek 1909, 351, Abb. 10, Taf. XXXIX, 2; Hurst 1975, 287–90.

46. Tomašević 1963, 22–3; Ulbert 1969, 38, Abb. 4.1 and Taf. 53.11; Ulbert 1970, 11, 43, Taf. 24.379.

47. In the stone barrack-blocks of auxiliary forts cross-divisions between the *contubernia* were probably sometimes of wood, as at

48. Pseudo-Hyginus, c.1; von Petrikovits 1975, 137. In the legionary barracks at Hod Hill the *contubernia* measured *c.* 3.65m by 3m or *c.* 3m by 2.45m, but there were no rooms adjoining the sleeping quarters for the storage of equipment as at Exeter and in other legionary barracks (Richmond 1968, 79, Fig.62).

49. Maxfield 1980, 304.

50. *EAR* (i), 7, following von Petrikovits 1975, 42.

51. Review of von Petrikovits 1975 in *Germania,* 55 (1977) 267.

52. A pair of barracks adjacent to those of the first cohort at Inchtuthil were thought to have accommodated 120 cavalry (I.A. Richmond in *J. Roman Stud.,* 51 (1961) 160). However, von Petrikovits (1975, 51) considered that the legionary cavalry were accommodated in *tabernae* in the *latera praetorii,* and along the *viae quintana* and *decumana.*

53. Manning 1975, 105.

54. Cunliffe 1968, 17–9, 236, Fig.10.

55. Von Petrikovits 1975, Bild 20.

56. Fox 1952, 31–7.

57. In the Augustan fortress at Haltern the *principia* were abutted on the north-east side (i.e. the sinistral side of the *latera praetorii*) by other buildings (von Schnurbein 1974, Beil. 1.).

58. The width of the *principia* is thus somewhat greater than that postulated in *EAR* (i), 9 (i.e. 45m). However, the *principia* at Exeter are still much smaller than most legionary examples (cf. von Petrikovits 1975, Bild 14).

59. The room which has been excavated is too large to have formed a *contubernium,* but the plans of the barracks of the first cohort were often irregular (e.g. Carnuntum and Lauriacum: von Petrikovits 1975, Bild 3) and the number of *contubernia* in each barrack-block sometimes varied (ibid., 41–2).

60. J.M.C. Toynbee in *EAR* (i), 130–2.

61. Boon 1972, 15; von Petrikovits (1975, 51) considered that the legionary cavalry were accommodated in *tabernae* (see n. 51).

62. That is, on the later *Insula II,* Site 1 and Insula *VII,* Site 1 and on Insula *XV* (Fig. 27).

63. *EAR* (i), 8.

64. *EAR* (i), 13–6.

65. *EAR* (i), Table 1.

66. *EAR* (i), 15–6.

67. Fox 1952, 53–4, Pl. XXV; Ralegh Radford and Morris 1933–6, 185; observations in the High Street (1974).

68. *EAR* (i), 192–3; *EAR* (iv), forthcoming.

69. Okehampton: Bidwell, Bridgwater and Silvester 1979, 257, Fig. 2B, 3; Nanstallon: Fox and Ravenhill 1972, Fig. 22, nos. 9, 11, 12; Carvossa: unpublished, pottery examined by kind permission of H. Miles and P. Carlyon, for the site see Douch and Beard 1970.

70. Mortaria, information from K. Hartley; *terra nigra,* see V. Rigby in *EAR* (i), 190, 221.

71. The fortress does not appear to have been supplied with pottery produced by local industries functioning in the immediately pre-Roman period; indeed such industries may not have existed.

72. See report by K.T. Greene in *EAR* (iv), forthcoming.

73. R.G. Scrivener in *EAR* (i), 135.

74. *EAR* (i), 9–11.

75. Fox 1968, 3–6.

76. Fox 1952, 51.

77. *EAR* (i), 11.

78. *EAR* (i), 11.

79. Shortt 1841, 91.

80. Fox and Ravenhill 1959, 71–82.

81. Fox 1974, 84–7.

82. Jarvis and Maxfield 1975, 210.

83. Ralegh Radford 1937–47, 10.

84. Maxfield 1980, 305–7, where it is stated that Topsham owed its development as a port in medieval times to the blocking of the river below Exeter by a weir. However, Topsham was of some importance as a port before the construction of the weir, as a study by A.M. Jackson (1972, 61) has shown.

Gelligaer: 'there may have been divisional walls of wood which have disappeared' (Ward 1903, 67).

IV. THE EARLY TOWN

Introduction

Recent excavations have shown that the town at Exeter retained not only most of the streets within the earlier fortress, but also its defences, which were not demolished until a much larger circuit was constructed in the late second century. The early development of the town has thus more in common with that of the *coloniae* at Gloucester and Colchester than with that of other Roman-British *civitas* capitals. In this chapter the topography of the early town is described, consideration is then given to the establishment of the Dumnonii as a *civitas peregrina,* and, finally, there is discussion about the character of the early town.

One result of the past nine years of excavation has been the recovery of a substantial part of the street-plan within the early town which allows the remainder to be reconstructed with a fair degree of certainty (Fig. 27). Accordingly, it is now possible to number the *insulae* within both the earlier and later town defences, although in the case of the latter (Fig. 37) the position of some streets is entirely conjectural (p. 47ff).

The reduction in size of the legionary baths

Before the erection of the *basilica* and *forum* in *c.* 80 (p. 49), but at a date within the Flavian period, considerable alterations were made to the legionary baths.[1] They are thought to have been occasioned by the departure of the legion in *c.* 75, and their significance is discussed on p. 56. The main result of the alterations was a reduction in size of the bath-house. The hypocaust in the *caldarium* was divided into two parts by the blocking of the channels which crossed its width at the centre. Above the hypocaust the room may have been divided by a timber screen; there are indications that the south-west part now served as the *caldarium,* and the north-east part as the *tepidarium.* In the former *tepidarium* the hypocaust was demolished and replaced by a mortar floor with a *terrazzo* finish; this room was probably now used as a *frigidarium.* A foundation which may have been the substructure of an unfinished bath was sealed below the floor. At a later date a series of post-holes and trenches was dug through the floor; they may have been associated with 'internal porches' constructed to eliminate heat-loss from the *caldarium* and *tepidarium* to the *frigidarium.*

In the *palaestra* a shallow footing may have been associated with the erection of a veranda or portico on the south-west side of the bath-house. Further alterations were made to the service-buildings.

The defences *(Figs. 9, 26)*

The later legionary ditch (p. 23) was filled in shortly after *c.* 80. In the trench at the southern corner of the defences (Fig. 9) there was a layer of silt *c.* 30cm in depth at the bottom of the ditch, above which the filling consisted of domestic refuse.[2] Elsewhere the ditch was filled with clay.

The discovery of a later ditch, which remained open until the late Antonine period, shows that the defences of the fortress were retained by the early town. The ditch was first noted in Mermaid Yard (1978) where it was 10m in width and 2m in depth and cut through the filling of the two earlier ditches (Fig. 26). The date at which it was dug is uncertain; the bottom cut a shallow scoop which may have represented yet another ditch, possibly a replacement of the later legionary ditch. The later civil ditch was also encountered at Rack Street and found to be 1.8m in depth with a width in excess of 9m.[3] In the trench at the southern corner of the defences the ditch was only 1.2m in depth and 5m in width. The upper levels on this site had been removed by medieval activities, but it seemed unlikely that the ditch was originally much larger; its dimensions may have been greatly reduced on the south-west side of the defences which ran along the crest of a steep slope.

In Mermaid Yard the outer face of the rampart (p. 23), which was preserved to a height of *c.* 90cm, was abutted by the layers of clay which filled the ditch (see below); the face was very weathered but no traces of collapse or repair were noted in the length of 9m which was examined.

Further traces of the early defences were found on the north-west side of the town near the former north-west gate of the fortress *(porta principalis sinistra).* The deep gully which was thought to have drained the legionary ditch (p. 23) was filled in after *c.* 75; another gully 2m in width and 1.2m in depth was dug just to the north-east and presumably drained a ditch associated with the civil phase of the defences.

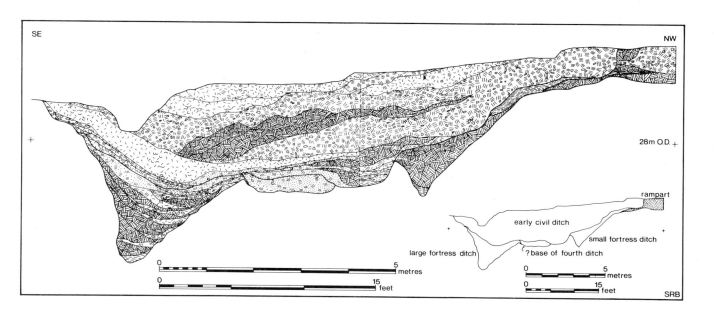

Fig. 26: Section across the defences of the legionary fortress and early town at Mermaid Yard (see Fig. 9).

The defences of the early town remained in use until the late Antonine period when they were superseded by a new circuit enclosing an area two and a half times greater (p. 59). The excavations have produced clear evidence for the neglect of the early defences prior to their demolition; the base of the ditch was covered with domestic refuse and three pits had been dug through its sides.[4] In Mermaid Yard the ditch was filled with deposits of clay which were almost certainly derived from the demolition of the rampart; this material formed a mound which in the last quarter of the third century was still a metre higher than the level of the street constructed immediately to the south-east.

The street-plan *(Figs. 27, 28)*

The early town adopted the street-plan of the fortress with few alterations. In the central area, which has been considered in detail elsewhere,[5] the *via principalis* was retained; it was divided into two parts by the *basilica* and *forum*, which occupied a double *insula* (XIII). The *via praetoria*, however, was replaced by a street 3m to the north-west which has been seen on the north-west sides of the *basilica* and *forum*[6] and *Insula* XIV. Between *Insulae* X and XIV this street was at least 15m in width, and no doubt served as a market-place, supplementing that on the south-west side of the *forum* (p. 52).

Excavation has established that the north-west and south-east parts of the *via sagularis* remained in use. On the north-west side of *Insula* II the former *via sagularis* was repaired twice following the destruction by fire of buildings on its north-west side in *c.* 80–85 (p. 53).[7] The *via sagularis* has also been sectioned on the south-east side of *Insula* XIX near the Speke Chapel and was found to have been resurfaced on one or possibly two occasions before it passed out of use (p. 24);[8] part of the same street was excavated south-east of *Insula* XV, but there only a few scraps of the original metalling survived later disturbance. In the part of the town north of the *basilica* and *forum* three of the four streets dividing the area into four *insulae* have been excavated. The street on the south-east side of *Insula* IV formerly bounding the south-east side of the *fabrica* (p. 31) continued in use throughout the Roman period, likewise the street on the south-east of *Insula V* which ran a little to the south-east. The street between *Insulae IV* and *V*, which formerly ran between the two barrack-blocks adjacent to the *fabrica* (p. 35), remained in use until the Hadrianic period. The street between *Insulae IX* and *X* has not yet been seen. East of the *basilica* and *forum* the streets on the north-west and north-east sides of *Insula XVIII* have been investigated; the former dates from the fortress[9] but nothing is known about the origins of the latter.[10]

A stretch of metalling beneath the south-west tower of the later second-century South Gate probably represents a predecessor of the street which passed through this gate.[11] This must formerly have been an extra-mural road leading to the south-east gate of the early town, which thus occupied a

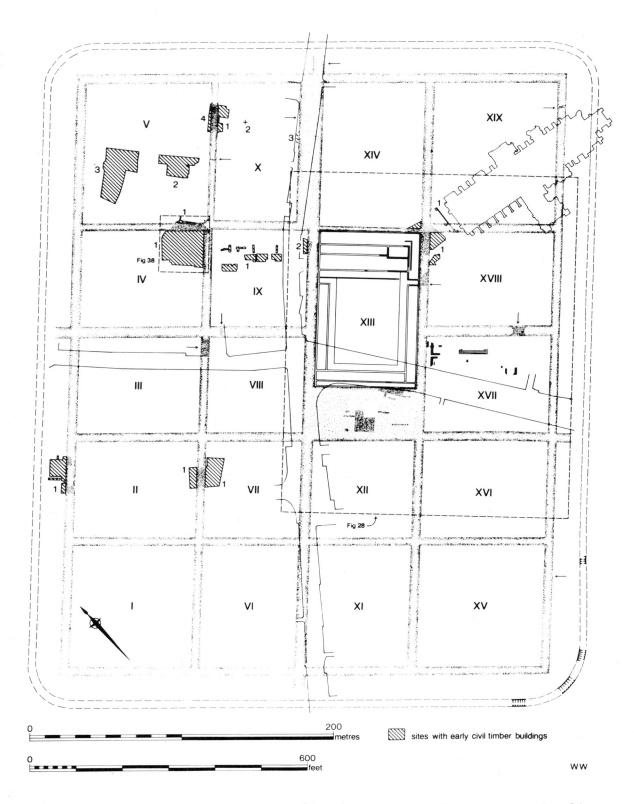

Fig. 27: The early town showing excavated sites with timber buildings (pp. 53–5). For a larger plan of the *basilica* and *forum* and adjacent *insulae*, see Fig. 28; for a larger plan of the sites on *Insulae* IV and V, see Fig. 38, 1. Arrows show position of sections across streets.

site 73m south-west of the south-east gate (*porta principalis dextra*) of the fortress. The site of the gate, which was presumably moved in *c.* 80, may have been altered in order to give direct access to the market-place in front of the *forum* by means of a street between *Insulae* XVI and XVII. This street has not yet been seen; it may possibly have been retained from the fortress. The street between *Insulae* III and VIII originated in the fortress, but the street between *Insulae* XIII and XVII may have been constructed in *c.* 80.[12] Little is known of the streets on the south-west side of the town, but nevertheless the plan of eight *insulae* can be reconstructed with a certain degree of confidence. The street between *Insulae* VI–VII and XI–XII occupies the presumed line of the *via decumana*. The street which divides the *insulae* from north-west to south-east is thought to represent a survival of the *via quintana* (the position of which is conjectural (p. 20)). The street between *Insulae* II and VII has been excavated and shown to overlie the post-trenches of fortress buildings.

The *basilica* and *forum* (Figs. 28, 29)

The outline plan of the *basilica* and *forum* can be reconstructed from information recovered during the course of excavations carried out in 1945–6 and 1971–7, and from observations made in 1912[13] (Fig. 28). The buildings occupied an area measuring 106.5m by 67m (7135.5 sq.m); the *basilica*, which incorporated part of the fabric of the earlier bath-house, was situated on the north-eastern side of the site; the *forum* extended across the line of the former *via principalis* and covered part of the site of the *principia*, and of the buildings to the south-east (probably the barracks of the first cohort (p. 38)).

After demolition of the south-west *caldarium* furnace-house and the portico on the north-east side of the *palaestra* was completed, a large timber building was erected on their sites. Much of this building lay outside the excavated area, but four post-pits, either for the supports of a ridge-pole or for aisle-posts, and a sleeper beam which is thought to have formed the south-east end wall were excavated; the south-west wall of the bath-house appears to have formed one of the side-walls of the building, which measured at least 15.6m by 8m. Its remains were sealed below the surface of the *forum*-courtyard and the south-east *forum*-portico; the building was thus in existence only during the construction of the *basilica* and *forum* (see further, p. 56).

On the site of the earlier bath-house the south-east wall of the *caldarium* and the north-east wall of the *caldarium*, *tepidarium*, and, no doubt, the *frigidarium* were retained to form the end and side walls of the *basilica* (Fig. 29); the hypocausts in the bath-house had been broken up and buried beneath layers of clay and rubble 1.2m in depth. The south-west wall of the *basilica* was newly constructed. At its south-east end there was a flight of steps which led up from the south-east *forum*-portico (see below), the floor of which was *c.* 40cm lower than that of the *basilica*. A flight of steps also appears to have run along the central portion of this wall, which was probably pierced by a series of arches giving access to the interior of the *basilica*; this arcade was closed off soon after or perhaps even during the construction of the *basilica* by the erection of a wall 4m to the south-west, which created an aisle or passage along the front of the *basilica*. The main body of the *basilica* was 10.4m in width, reducing to 9m in width at its south-east end; its overall length must have been no greater than 60m.

To the north-east of the *basilica* there was a range of rooms which would have accommodated administrative offices and probably a shrine dedicated to the tutelary deity of the town. Only the room at the south-east end of the range has been completely excavated. It measured 13m by 7.6m; its north-west wall, in addition to those on the north-east and south-east sides of the room, was retained from the legionary baths. Its size and proportions suggests that it was the *curia* (meeting-place of the *ordo decurionum*); seating for the decurions would have run down the length of the room on either side of a central gangway and there would have been a rostrum for the presiding magistrate at one end of the room. On the south-east side of the *basilica* there was a passage which was continued along the north-east side in the form of a veranda or portico. The narrow areas between the passage and veranda and the boundary walls next to the streets on the north-east and south-east sides of the *insula* remained open until the late second century; the south-eastern boundary wall was retained from the legionary baths.

The eastern corner of the *forum*-courtyard has been examined and found to have had a mortar surface. In the western corner of the excavated area a cross-shaped feature was cut through the surface; it was composed of four trenches *c.* 1.05–1.25m in length and *c.* 30–50cm in width, but with a uniform depth of 15cm. The four arms of the cross probably held beams to which cross-struts supporting an upright pole may have been secured; a similar feature was found in the orchestra of the theatre at Verulamium and was thought perhaps to have been 'a maypole, gibbet or post to which baited beasts could be chained'.[14] The *forum*-courtyard was separated from the street by a portico and a range of rooms. The latter was pierced by a passage 3.1m in width with a monumental entry

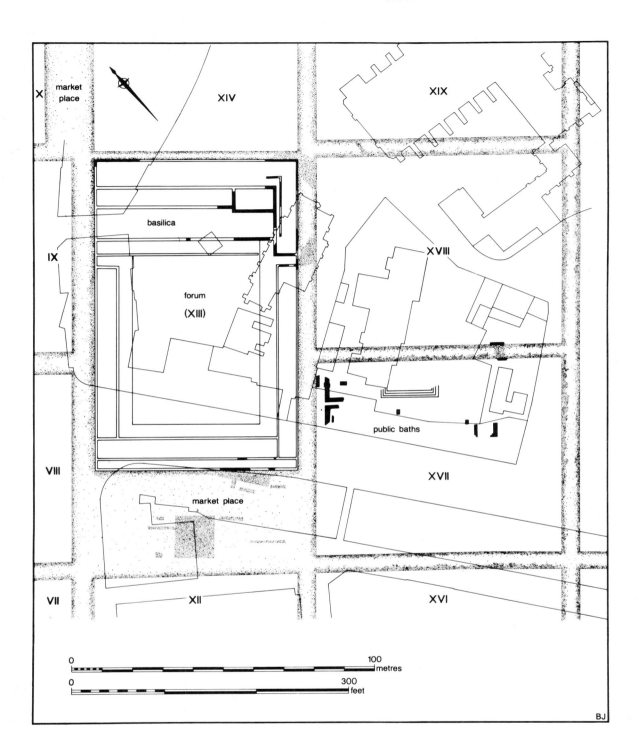

Fig. 28: The *basilica* and *forum* and the public baths with surrounding *insulae*. Heavy stippling shows metalling of streets and market-places revealed by excavation.

reached from the street by two steps. On its north-east side there was a room measuring 6.2m by *c.* 3.75m with an entry 3.2m wide which gave onto the passage. On the south-west side of the entry there was another room 6.08m in width and at least 6.6m in length; access to the *forum*-portico was gained from an entry on the north-west side of the room. The *forum*-portico was *c.* 5.5m in width, and consisted of a colonnade which probably supported a wooden architrave. The base of the terminal

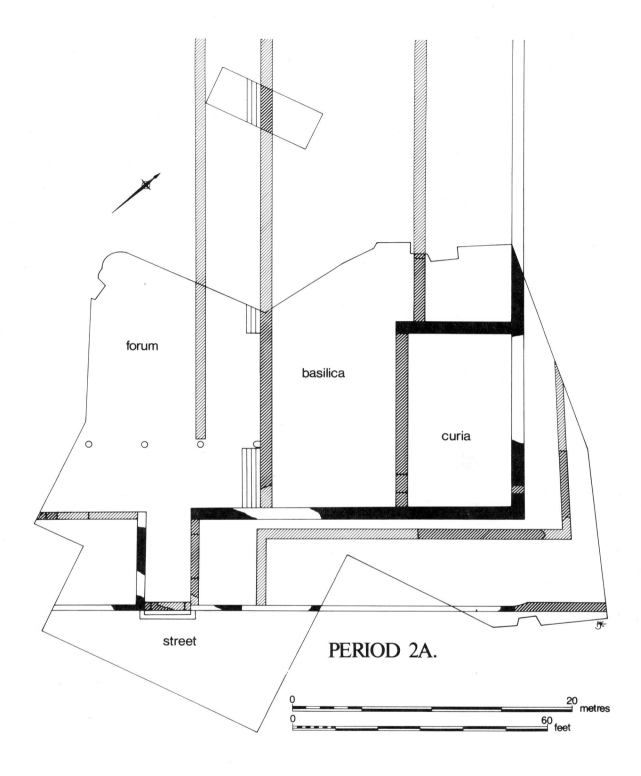

forum

basilica

curia

street

PERIOD 2A.

0   20 metres
0   60 feet

Fig. 29: Eastern corner of the *basilica* and *forum* constructed in *c.* 80. Walls in black retained from the legionary baths.

column survived on the north-west side of the steps which led up to the *basilica*. A stone gutter along the front of the colonnade collected water from its roof: the gutter emptied into a stone-lined drain which ran below the floor of the passage to the south-east, flowing into a wooden water-pipe below the street. Another branch of the drain terminated in the room on the north-east side of the passage, and may have collected water from the roof of the *basilica*.

Fig. 30: Pavement of sandstone slabs surrounding pool of public baths under the garden of the Deanery. Reproduced by permission of the Devon Archaeological Society.

Observations in 1912 recorded the position of two walls which represent the northern corner of the *basilica* and *forum*. In 1945–6 two parallel walls were located, which can now be seen to have represented an external portico on the south-west side of the *forum*. Beyond the portico there was an open metalled area measuring *c.* 67m by 32m, which can be identified as a market-place (another market-place appears to have been situated on the south-east side of *Insula X* (p. 47).

Deposits associated with the construction of the *basilica* and *forum* and with the demolition of the underlying legionary baths contained a sizeable group of finds: there was a number of samian vessels which were Flavian in date, including two manufactured after *c.* 75, and four coins of Vespasian, two of *c.* 71 and the others of *c.* 72–3, one of the latter a well-circulated issue. The evidence for the construction-date of the *basilica* and *forum* at Exeter would fit very well with Agricola's promotion of such undertakings in 79–80.

The public baths *(Figs. 28, 30)*

The public baths were situated on *Insula* XVII on the south-east side of the *basilica* and *forum* (Fig. 28).[15] Several chance discoveries of walls and tessellated pavements have been recorded on their site since the 1830s. The only extensive excavations yet undertaken have revealed a *piscina* or pool which was *c.* 1.0m in depth, *c.* 16.75m in length and of unknown width;[16] the *piscina* was surrounded by a pavement of sandstone slabs *c.* 2.5m in width with a shallow gutter cut down its centre (Fig. 30). A column-base was found on the floor of the *piscina*, and traces 'of the position occupied by similar columns' were said to have been found on the inner edge of the pavement; it is possible that the *piscina* was surrounded by a free-standing colonnade, its purpose purely decorative. In 1945–6 a room represented by a wall running from south-west to north-east with a return to the south-east was excavated on the north-west side of the *insula;*[17] these walls cut levels containing finds of the fortress period and may date to the late first century. No certain traces of the main bathing-suite have come to light, but massive foundations encountered under South Street may have formed part of its sub-structures; the axis of the suite probably ran from north-west to south-east in order to give the *caldarium* the customary southern aspect.

There is little evidence for the construction-date of the baths, but they may well have been erected at the same time as the *basilica* and *forum.*

Domestic occupation within the defences

In this section timber buildings within the defences of the early town are catalogued and discussed; some may date to the period after the erection of the later defensive circuit but are considered here with the earlier buildings. On many sites at Exeter levels of this period were extensively disturbed by later Roman and subsequent activities with the result that it has not yet proved possible to retrieve a complete plan of any building. Nevertheless, most of the buildings appear to be simple rectangular structures, a type familiar from other Romano-British towns.

These buildings display a variety of construction-techniques:

i) post-trench construction: this was the technique employed for all the buildings within the fortress, but is encountered much less frequently in the early town.

ii) sill-beam construction: this is the most common technique. The sill-beams were sometimes laid in shallow trenches but often directly on the ground surface, their presence detectable only where floor levels abutted them.

iii) other techniques: these include buildings represented by a series of post-pits, and others where sill-beams were laid on shallow stone footings.

The floors of these buildings were usually of clay or earth, but sometimes of lime- or brick-mortar. A large pile of black and white *tesserae* were found in a house on *Insula* V, and individual *tesserae* are frequent finds in levels of this period. A number of these houses also had painted wall-plaster. The roofs were covered with clay tiles, sometimes perhaps with wooden shingles; in the later second century Devon slate came into use (p. 81).

To judge from the excavations carried out so far, the street-frontages were densely built up, and the town must have accommodated a substantial population from its earliest years.

GAZETTEER OF BUILDINGS WITHIN THE EARLY TOWN *(Fig. 27)*

Intervallum north-east of *Insula II:* (1) two timber buildings, one measuring 7.3m by 6.7m, the other 8.5m by 7.0m were excavated; possible traces of a third were also found. An interim account[18] dated their construction to *c.* 65–70 and their destruction by fire to *c.* 80–85. It is possible that these were fortress buildings which survived in use in the early town, but their construction-date may fall after *c.* 75 (see p. 24). Following their destruction the site remained vacant although the street continued in use.

Insula II: (1) on the south-east side of this *insula* a later Roman masonry building was preceded by at least four successive timber buildings, the earliest contemporary with the original street surface on the south-east side of this *insula*, which was laid down immediately above the fortress buildings.

Insula IV: (1) a site excavated on the eastern corner of this *insula* remained open for a decade or so after *c.* 75, although slight remains of buildings excavated to the north-west may date to the late first century. A well which may once have been timber-lined was dug next to the street corner; its filling contained the Purbeck marble torso of an eagle (p. 38) and a group of 23 samian vessels closed by three Dr. 37s dating to *c.* 80–100. Another well was found further north-west; it was *c.* 3m in depth, square in plan and lined with wooden slats secured to uprights at the corners (Fig. 31). At a date between the end of the first century and the Hadrianic period a timber building was erected on the site (Fig. 38, 1); it was destroyed by fire at the same time as the building on the opposite side of the street in *Insula* V (see below). *Insulae* IV and V were subsequently amalgamated and the street between them was built over; the occupation on *Insula* IV/V is discussed below.

Insula V: (1) at the south corner of this *insula* the fragmentary remains of three successive timber buildings were excavated; they dated from *c.* 75 to the Hadrianic period. The last of these buildings (Fig. 38, 1) was destroyed by a fire which also consumed the building on *Insula* IV (see above). The

Fig. 31: Timber-lined well on *Insula* IV, site 1.2m scale.

street between *Insulae* IV and V was covered with burnt daub from the destruction of the buildings, above which were dumps of clay containing Hadrianic samian. Three successive timber buildings were subsequently erected on the north-east side of the site (see Fig. 38, 2 and 3 for the penultimate and ultimate buildings), and at least one on the south-west side.

(2) on this site early civil activities were represented by hearths and occupation levels, but buildings were not erected until after *c.* 90, and perhaps not until the second quarter of the second century. On the south-west side of the site there were five successive timber buildings, two erected before the end of the second century and three before the mid to late third century when the last of these was demolished and replaced by a large masonry building (p. 71). Traces of earlier timber buildings were also recovered below a masonry building on the north-east side of the site (p. 71).

(3) on this site, which extended to within 12m of the street behind the defences, the only signs of occupation in the later first and second centuries were a small number of rubbish pits.

(4) traces of timber buildings at the side of the street were found immediately above the fortress levels.

Insula VII: (1) a timber building was erected shortly after the street was constructed in *c.* 80 (p. 49). It was destroyed by fire and at least three successive timber buildings had been erected on its site before the construction of a masonry building in the later Roman period (p. 72).

Insula IX: (1) traces of three successive timber buildings were found above the fortress levels. A masonry building was erected on their site after *c.* 270.

(2) four post-pits formed part of a building which had encroached on the street; traces of a timber building, possibly the same as that represented by the post-pits, were seen nearby in a section exposed by the collapse of a cellar wall.[19]

Insula X: (1) part of a substantially constructed building was found immediately above the fortress levels. Its frontage onto the street was at least 17.5m in length, and it appeared to have been divided into a series of rooms *c.* 2.4m in width and at least 4.5m in length. It was cut by the post-trenches of another timber building which was demolished in the first half of the second century. The site then remained free of buildings until the later third century (p. 73).

(2) a well *c.* 4.5m in depth and lined with trap blocks was revealed during building work. Its waterlogged contents dated to the late second century and included a wooden bowl, comb, shovel, barrel-staves and a fragment of a rush mat or basket.

(3) floor-levels associated with timber buildings were noted in the course of building work. *Insula* XVIII: (1) a timber building was erected on the north-west side of this *insula* when the legionary baths were reduced in size *c.* 75; it was demolished when the *basilica* and *forum* were erected in *c.* 80.[20] Floor levels associated with later timber buildings were also found; one of these was destroyed by fire in the late second or early third centuries.[21]

Insula XIX: (1) traces of timber buildings were recovered.[22]

Extra-mural occupation *(Fig. 24)*

Excavations have recovered evidence of occupation on a considerable scale beyond the defences of the early town.

Outside the north-east gate: the substantial post-trenches of a timber building were found at 228, High Street above the road which may have skirted the fortress ditch (p. 23). Its construction resembled that of the late first-century building on *Insula* X, site 1 (see above). South-east of the road leading to the gate second-century pits were found on *Insula* XXVII, sites 1 and 2.[23] Beneath the mosaics of a late Roman town-house on *Insula* XXII, site 1 (p. 73) a stretch of metalling 40cm thick and 7.3m in width was found running from north-west to south-east. Three pieces of samian, the latest of mid second-century date, were sealed beneath its surface.[24] Further to the south-east on *Insula* XXIV, site 1 a street was sectioned;[25] it probably represents a continuation of the metalling found on *Insula* XXII, site 1. There were three layers of metalling, the second containing early second-century pottery. This street may have originated during the fortress period, but it continued in use until the mid second century at the earliest. It may have gone out of use when the street-system was replanned in the later second century following the erection of the new defensive circuit (p. 67).

In 1836 a 'Roman Sepulchral Vault' was found behind the Three Tuns Inn, in High Street; if this is a *columbarium* (which is open to question),[26] domestic occupation could not have spread very far along the road from the north-east gate of the early town.

Outside the south-east gate: the *porta principalis dextra* of the fortress was apparently superseded by a gate further to the south-west at the head of a street leading to the market-place in front of the *forum* (pp. 47–8). The metalling of the road leading to the gate was seen beneath the south-west tower of the later Roman South Gate. Nearby was found a metal-working hearth, probably associated with the cupellation of silver from lead or copper alloys, which can be dated to the mid second century.[27] Excavations beyond the later defences revealed traces of second-century occupation on both sides of the Roman road. The area to the north-east was divided by shallow ditches into a series of small plots. In the mid second century the ditches were levelled and a roughly metalled track *c.* 8m in width was laid down; it approached the road leading to the south-east gate at an oblique angle, and seemed to be heading roughly northwards to the area beyond the north-east gate, perhaps by-passing the town by linking the Fosse Way and the road to Topsham (Fig. 36). The track was remetalled with clay and gravel on three occasions, and each surface was deeply rutted; it went out of use at the end of the second century, possibly when the new defences were erected. On the south-west side of the road the civil Roman levels had been truncated in the seventeenth century, but a few post-trenches on a slightly different alignment to those of the earlier military buildings were found; one contained second-century pottery. Pits of this period were also found, as well as two successive ditches which may have been associated with the road to Topsham.

Outside the south-west gate: on the later *Insula XXX*, on a site about 70m from the western corner of the defences, part of a timber building was found; its floor-levels contained pottery of Flavian-

Trajanic date. A pottery workshop was established nearby in the late Neronian or early Flavian period, and may have continued in production during the earliest years of the town (p. 41).

Outside the north-west gate: no excavations have been carried out on this side of the town apart from a section cut through the later defences, where no traces of occupation levels were found below the bank.

The establishment of a civilian administration

The fortress at Exeter was abandoned in c. 75. but the foundation of the *civitas peregrina* may not have taken place until c. 80 when work on the *basilica* and *forum* commenced (see below). If, as seems probable, the transfer of the legion to Caerleon was accompanied by the withdrawal of garrisons from the forts in the South-West, there would have been an interregnum of some five years, when the affairs of the *civitas* may have been the responsibility of a *praefectus civitatis,* an officer appointed by the governor;[28] prominent natives were also sometimes appointed to similar positions.[29] There is no direct evidence for the existence of such posts in Britain, but they are attested in many other provinces. The alterations to the legionary baths were probably made during this period (p. 46). The bathing-suite was considerably reduced in size, and the remainder of the site may have been put to other uses. The *palaestra,* for example, may have served as a market-place and the former *frigidarium* could have served as a market-hall. The timber hall erected on the site of the *palaestra* during the construction of the *basilica* and *forum* perhaps provided temporary accommodation for the commercial life of the town.

In the absence of building inscriptions the construction of public buildings, especially the *basilica* and *forum*, is thought to provide the best indication of the date at which a grant of self-government was made to a *civitas peregrina*.[30] On these grounds we would be justified in concluding that the *civitas Dumnoniorum* passed from military control, perhaps after a brief period of administration by a *praefectus civitas* or a similar official (see above), to self-government in c. 80 (p. 52). The establishment of the *civitas peregrina* and construction of public buildings may well have resulted from Agricola's policy of Romanisation in 79–80. He is said by Tacitus to have promoted the construction of 'temples, market-places *(fora)* and houses.'[31]

Having discussed the date at which a grant of self-government was made, the structure of the administration which was set up at that time can now be examined. Very little information about local government in Britain has come to light, but the administration of the *civitas peregrina* can be reconstructed by reference to practice in other western provinces of the Empire. The *civitas* would be governed by an *ordo decurionum,* a council usually one hundred in number, although smaller memberships are known.[32] The qualifications for enrolment in the *ordo* were based on the value of property held by the candidate; it generally had to amount to 100,000 *sesterces,* but sometimes lesser sums were required.[33] Two pairs of magistrates, the *duoviri iuridicundo* and the *aediles*, were appointed annually by the *ordo.*

The *civitas* was probably divided into a number of *pagi*. C. Thomas has suggested tentatively that the hundreds of Cornwall may have preserved the boundaries of the *pagi* to some degree.[34] The Cornish hundreds were once probably six in number, although later divided to form nine, and there are hints that they are of pre-English origin. Thomas considered that the large size and poor internal communications of the *civitas Dumnoniorium* would have made the existence of administrative sub-divisions such as *pagi* likely, and that their boundaries would be drawn to take account of cultural differences within the local population at the beginning of the Roman period. For example, the limited and broadly similar distribution of fogous and courtyard-houses, both apparently of pre-Roman origin, can be associated with a distinctive group of Celtic people confined to West Penwith; their territory may have received formal recognition as a *pagus* within the *civitas.*[35]

Any settlement of appreciable size within the *civitas* would have become a *vicus,* enabling the inhabitants to form a council and elect magistrates. The *civitas* capital at Exeter was probably also a *vicus* with an administration distinct from, but subordinate to, that of the *civitas;*[36] this distinction was probably of little account, at least during the later first and early second centuries when most of the decurions would probably have been resident within the town (p. 57).

The character of the early town

The closest parallels for the development of the early town at Exeter are to be found not among other *civitas* capitals in Britain but in the first-century *coloniae* at Gloucester and Colchester.[37] Here, as at

Exeter, the plans of earlier fortresses were adapted to serve the needs of the towns which were established on their sites. As we have already seen (p. 13), the defences and street-plan of the fortress at Gloucester were retained by the *colonia,* and even the boundaries of earlier building plots were respected by the first civilian buildings to be erected; at Colchester the defences of the fortress were levelled when the *colonia* was founded, but many of the streets remained in use and parts of some barracks were still standing at the time of the Boudican rebellion.[38] It is well known that most of the principal Romano-British towns were established on earlier military sites,[39] but it is only at Exeter and in the *coloniae* that we find towns which are adaptations of these earlier military establishments (although the *civitas* capital at Wroxeter may prove to be another example).

At the sites of other towns, especially in south-east Britain, these earlier establishments were small forts held for brief periods. For example, at Verulamium a fort (*c.* 2ha in area) was founded *c.* 43 in the neighbourhood of a native *oppidum* and was held for about six years. Such a small fort was not likely to have been associated with an extensive *vicus,* and the establishment of a town on its site can be attributed to the possibility that a *praefectus civitatis* (p. 56) had used the fort as an administrative headquarters,[40] to its position in the road-system of the province and to the nearby presence of a large population in the native *oppidum.*

The retention of the legionary defences also makes Exeter a special case. Most towns in Roman Britain were not provided with defences until the later second century (p. 66), and special circumstances operated in the cases of those that were. The *coloniae* at Gloucester and Lincoln retained the defences of earlier fortresses on their sites because their function was partly military and removal of the fortress defences at Colchester, established as a *colonia* in *c.* 49, had laid it open to the onslaught of rebels in 61.[41] Verulamium was probably equipped with defences because of its status as a *municipium.*[42] The outer earthwork at Silchester is thought to have been erected at the time of the Boudican rebellion;[43] the defences at Winchester, which may have formed a part of Cogidubnus' kingdom along with Silchester, date from *c.* 70.[44]

A factor common to all these defended towns is their undoubted loyalty to Roman rule. The retention of the fortress defences at Exeter thus supplies some evidence that the population was judged to be strongly philo-Roman. Their retention may also suggest that the town was thought liable to attack, although whether by the Dumnonii, or at least a section of that tribe, or by more distant enemies is uncertain. Although the general lack of Romanisation in most parts of the *civitas* Dumnoniorum may partly be explained by the poverty of the population, it also hints at indifference, if not outright hostility, to Roman rule. The disparity of development between Exeter and its hinterland can be contrasted with events in parts of south-east Britain where the growth of towns and of villa estates in the countryside marched *pari passu.* Indeed, in the first and early second centuries there are signs that progress in the countryside may have outstripped that in towns: for example it has recently been argued that the architecture of villas provided the prototypes for the plans of town-houses.[45] Most of these early villas were probably owned by tribal notables who rapidly took advantage of the material benefits of conquest; we would expect that many qualified for membership of the *ordo,* took part in the political life of their *civitas* and acquired residence within the towns. There are few signs of similar developments in the South-West. The only villa known to the west of Exeter is at Magor, near Camborne;[46] It was occupied between the mid second and mid third centuries. Two villa-sites very close to, or possibly beyond, the eastern border of the *civitas* at Holcombe[47] and Seaton[48] were occupied from the first century.[49]

Two sources which the population of the early town at Exeter could have drawn upon are the inhabitants of the earlier *canabae* and natives within the *civitas.* Given the lack of Romanisation within the *civitas,* the possibility that at least some sections of the Dumnonii remained indifferent or even hostile to Roman rule and the indications that the early town was strongly philo-Roman, it seems likely that the more important of these two sources was the *canabae,* the population of which would have consisted largely of traders and veterans. The early town was the only centre of Romanisation within the *civitas,* and its inhabitants were likely to have formed a majority of the decurions. Most of its population may have depended for a living on the cultivation of land in the vicinity, and contact between the town and many parts of the *civitas* may have been rare (for the evidence of trade, see pp. 80–1). Exeter had little effect on conditions of life within the *civitas* as a whole, and remained an outpost of Romano-British society in a zone where the effects of the Roman conquest are scarcely perceptible.

NOTES

1. *EAR* (i), 60–6.
2. See *EAR* (i), 187–8, Table 9. The deposit contained 38 samian vessels, all of Flavian or Neronian-Flavian date. The latest piece was a Dr. 37 of *c*. 80–100, and there were 13 more Dr. 37 bowls, eight of Flavian date, four dating to *c*. 75–90 and one to *c*. 70–85; only two Dr. 29 bowls were found (*c*. 75–90 and *c*. 60–80); there was also a Dr. 30 (*c*. 60–80) and a stamp (*c*. 65–90). This deposit seemed to be entirely free of residual material and contained large quantities of food bones and oyster shells. The filling in the other sections contained a Dr. 29 (*c*. 70–90), two Flavian and two other first-century vessels, and one Neronian piece.
3. When this feature was first seen at Rack Street, it was thought to have formed part of the later legionary ditch, thus giving rise to the erroneous statement that the latter cut the earlier fortress ditch (*EAR* (i), 3).
4. The pits and domestic refuse contained samian of Antonine and late-Antonine date; the period of neglect may not have long ante-dated the construction of the new defensive circuit.
5. *EAR* (i), 78–80. The street shown south-east of *Insulae* XVII and XVIII in ibid., Fig. 22, probably dates to the late second century (p. 67); in the early town these *insulae* are now thought to have been bounded by the south-east part of the *via sagularis*.
6. *EAR* (i), 120.
7. Fox 1966, 49.
8. Morris 1933–6, 229, Pl.LIV. There were four layers of trap spalls and gravel with an overall thickness of 40cm, which apparently represented two layers of make-up and two street-surfaces. Above there was another layer of make-up 'with a patch of pebbles having the appearance of a channel or paving'; this may be another street-surface or a floor associated with the masonry building which was built over the street (p. 76).
9. *EAR* (i), 26.
10. ibid., 118.
11. Fox 1968, 6.
12. It was seen in 1945–6 and found to consist of 'a well-compacted 4in (10cm) layer of fine gravel resting on the natural soil' (Fox 1952, 43, Pl.XVI); it crossed the probable site of the barrack-blocks for the first cohort.
13. For the recent excavations and a re-evaluation of older work, see *EAR* (i), 67–90.
14. Kenyon 1935, 281 and Pls. 60,2 and 68.
15. See *EAR* (i), 121–3 for a full discussion.
16. Montgomerie-Neilson and Montague 1933–6, 72–8.
17. Fox 1952a, 42–4.
18. Fox 1966, 49.
19. *EAR* (i), 120–1.
20. ibid., 64.
21. ibid., 115–7.
22. ibid., 118.
23. Fox 1952, 49–50.
24. ibid., 47, Pl.XXIV, Sect. A–B. The metalling was *c*. 45cm thick and may have included one or more resurfacings not noted at the time of excavation.
25. ibid., 51–2, Pl.XIXD and Pl.XXIV.
26. Described as a 'Roman family Sepulchral Vault, seven foot square, arched over, and containing five coarse strongly baked cinerary Urns, arranged in niches around its interior' (Shortt 1840, 142); a skull was found 'at some distance from the Urns'. R.G. Goodchild (in Fox 1952, 103) thought it was a pottery kiln, perhaps of medieval date, but Collingwood and Richmond (1969, 167) accepted its identification as a *columbarium*. Another example is known from White Notley in Essex. It took the form of a circular brick-built tomb 2.45m across with a chamber 1.15m square with three niches in its walls (*VCH (Essex)* III, 164, Pl.LXXXIVB). At Pleshey in the same county (ibid., 166) a vault about 3m square was found in the eighteenth century; its sides were formed into niches containing urns filled with bones.
27. Road and metal-working hearth, see Fox 1968. The base and sides of the hearth were lined with heavily burnt animal bones; analysis showed that there was one per cent of lead in some pieces.
28. Rivet 1977, 171.
29. Wilkes 1969, 287–8; Mócsy 1974, 134.
30. Frere 1978, 235.
31. Tacitus, *Agricola*, 21, 1.
32. Abbott and Johnson 1926, 65.
33. ibid., 166.
34. Thomas 1964, 70–4.
35. Fox 1973, 182.
36. J.E. Bogaers in *J. Roman Stud.*, 57 (1967) 231–3.
37. The early town at Exeter can also be compared with the *vicus* which was established in the fortress at Vindonissa after the departure of the Eleventh Legion in 101. Here the legionary baths were still standing in the second half of the second century when they were reduced in size. The fortress defences may also have been in use during the period of the *vicus*; some authorities believe that the west gate was rebuilt at this time (for recent discussion, see Ettlinger 1972, 16, 18–19).
38. In Numidia *coloniae* were established in the former fortress of the Third Augustan Legion at Theveste and Ammaedara during the second half of the first century, but nothing as yet is known of the relationships between the plans of the fortresses and early towns (Fentress 1979, 126).
39. Webster 1966.
40. Rivet 1977, 171. The later *basilica* and *forum* at Verulamium cover the site of the fort almost exactly, although their respective axes differ by a few degrees (Frere 1972, Fig. 2); this might be taken to indicate that the fort was the seat of an earlier administration.
41. Tacitus, *Annals*, XIV, 32; Crummy 1977, 87.
42. Frere 1964, 104.
43. Boon 1974, 46, but see now *Britannia*, 10 (1979) 331.
44. Biddle 1970, 284. For the possible extent of Cogidubnus' territories see Barrett 1979, 230–4 and Bogaers 1979, 253.
45. Walthew 1975.
46. O'Neill 1934.
47. Pollard 1977.
48. Miles 1977; Silvester forthcoming.
49. In addition to these villa-sites possible indications of the existence of Romanised buildings elsewhere in Devon are provided by the discovery of a roofing tile at Dartington Hall (in the collection of the Devon Centre, information J.P. Allan) and the finds of box-tiles with combing-marks from excavations at Totnes Castle (Rigold 1954, 250) and from unpublished excavations on a medieval town-site at Exmouth (information P. Weddell). Trenches for the construction of a barn on the site of Newenham Abbey near Axminster showed that the make-up levels for the floor of the church incorporated many Roman tiles of various types, presumably from the remains of a nearby building (information R.J. Silvester). Roofing tiles from an excavation on reclaimed land at Sutton Pool, the medieval harbour of Plymouth, may have come from a masonry building (*Archaeol. Review*, 1 (1966) 34). However, another possibility is that they are from a boat; tiles which clearly did not form part of the cargo are often found in wrecks of the classical period, and are thought to have been used for hearths and the roofs of galleys (cook-houses) as a protection against fire (Casson 1971, 178n. 52).

V. THE LATER TOWN DEFENCES

Introduction

The later town defences, the only remains of Roman Exeter still visible, enclosed an area of 37ha (92.6 acres) by means of a wall 2.35km (1.45 miles) in circuit. These defences were retained by both the late Saxon and medieval towns, and until well into the last century the greater part of the population of Exeter lived within the walls. Seventy per cent of the circuit still survives, although the external facing of the wall has been replaced in medieval and later times, and short stretches completely rebuilt. The Roman wall was probably *c.* 6m in height with a walk-way and parapet above. At its rear there was an earth bank at least 6m in width which may or may not pre-date the wall. There were four gates, and the existence of a fifth at the southern corner giving access to a quay is very likely, although unproven.

The course of the new circuit was no doubt determined by tactical considerations and the need to enclose built-up areas outside the old defences. Rougemont was included within the new defences, as was also a considerable area beyond the former north-east and south-east gates of the town. At the southern corner the defences passed across the bottom of the Coombe valley and then crossed the steep slope above the Exe beyond the West Gate. On the north-west side the defences followed the crest of the precipitous slope above the Longbrook.

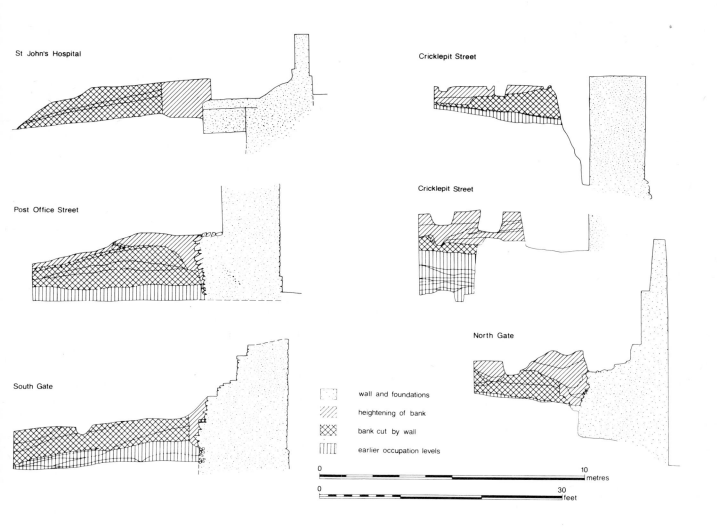

Fig. 32: Simplified sections across the defences of the later town. For their general location, see Fig. 1.

The bank *(Figs. 32–4)*

Thirteen separate excavations have been carried out on the defences since 1932.[1] In every trench where more than just the foundations of the wall are preserved the following sequence of construction has been observed: earlier occupation-levels are covered by a bank consisting of redeposited natural sub-soil mixed with lenses of domestic refuse; the foundations of the wall have been inserted, cutting the front of the bank; the wall has then been built up to its full height and the bank heightened to form a rampart behind the wall.

The existence of the bank was first noted in 1935 at St John's School[2] where it was 1.2m in height and at least 5.4m in width. It was also preserved to its full height at Bedford Circus (1.6m),[3] South Gate (1.4m), Cricklepit Street (70cm in one trench, 1.2m in the other)[4] and North Gate (1.05m). Excavation in the Palace Garden showed that the bank extended back for a distance of 6m from the inner face of the wall,[5] but at the South Gate its width exceeded 6.5m.[6] In each of these sections the front of the bank had been cut back just beyond its crest when the wall foundations were inserted; the rear of the bank sloped back gently to the original ground-surface. The material employed in its construction was the natural subsoil (clay or gravel) mixed with occupation-debris, and no doubt derived from digging the ditch beyond the defences.[7] The bank differed markedly from the legionary rampart where clay blocks retained a filling of horizontal layers of compacted clay (p. 23).

The bank has long been considered to represent an independent phase of the defences, which were later strengthened by the addition of a wall.[8] If so, this first phase of the defences took the form of a bank and ditch of a type common during the Iron Age, although also found in the early Roman period at Silchester in the Outer and Inner Earthworks.[9] It is certain that the low, gently-sloping bank does not represent the remains of a levelled rampart of Roman military type; a sufficient number of trenches has been cut through the bank to show that a rear revetment, whether of clay, turf or timber, never existed.

Another interpretation of the function of the bank is possible: it may merely represent the up-cast from the digging of a defensive ditch and from the foundation-trench of the wall itself. The face of the bank would be trimmed back when the wall-foundations were inserted, and then the bank would be heightened to form a rampart when the wall was completed. At Bedford Circus the surface of the bank was covered by a layer of 'black soil containing many pieces of charcoal' which was thought to represent a turf-line;[10] but in the recent excavations at Cricklepit Street and North Gate (Fig. 33) there was only a thin layer of trampled grit on the surface of the bank. The 'black soil' at Bedford Circus may well have been redeposited.

Substance is lent to this interpretation by excavations carried out on the defences of Aldborough in Yorkshire. At three points on the western side of the defences a bank which preceded the construction of the wall was traced. In Section III there was a layer of dirty sand a metre thick which ended abruptly about 5m from the wall; the gap was filled when the wall was constructed.[11] At the north-west corner at a distance of 25m from Section III it was found that the wall cut through a bank of sand 1.8m in height.[12] Recent work by D. Charlesworth on the east and west sides of the defences has again established the existence of a bank of sand 1–1.2m in height preceding construction of the wall; in both sections the bank in fact sealed the edge of the wall-foundation, but D. Charlesworth has pointed out that this may have resulted from the collapse of the front of the bank which here as elsewhere consisted of sand.[13] It is impossible, however, to concur with the argument that this bank represents an independent phase of the defences. D. Charlesworth overlooks a section cut across the northern defences in the course of earlier excavations which established the contemporaneity of the wall and rampart.[14] Here a bank of sand over-sailed the foundations of the wall for a width of 90cm; it was clear from the incline of tip-lines within the bank that the material had been piled against the rear of the wall and had not slipped forward from the front of an already existing bank, as may have happened elsewhere (see above). The absence of a bank preceding construction of the wall at this point is of no significance if the bank merely resulted from the disposal of soil dug from the ditch, but is quite inexplicable if the bank is thought to have had a defensive function.[15]

On the other hand, some Romano-British towns were certainly equipped with earthwork defences in the later second century. The best example is perhaps at Dorchester-on-Thames[16] where there was a rampart built of turves, its base reinforced with timber strapping, a mode of construction familiar from the defences of Roman forts and fortresses. There is also an undoubted example at Silchester:

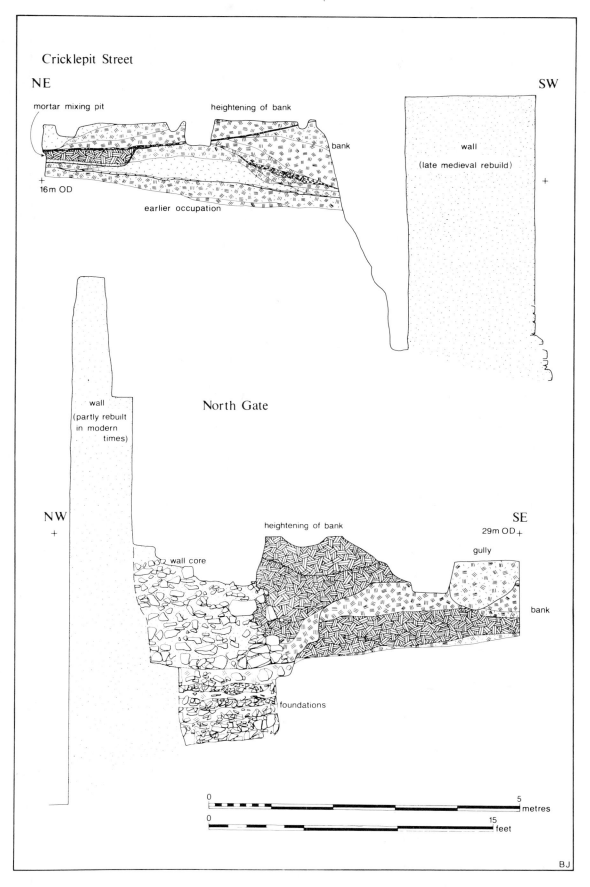

Fig. 33: Sections across the defences of the later town at Cricklepit Street and North Gate. For their general location, see Fig. 3.

Fig. 34: Section through the later town defences at North Gate. Left, back of stone wall; foreground, bank thrown up before construction of wall; top, heightening of bank which took place after construction of wall. 2m scale.

beneath the main bank was a setting-out bank showing 'the reverse sequence of stratification that would exist at the time a ditch was dug'; the main bank was built of 'sandy clay deliberately laced with flat gravel bonding-layers', and its height was 2.5m.[17] At Cirencester the defences have been explored at a number of points,[18] and the bank was found to be up to 3m in height; it appears that work had been started on masonry fortifications and then abandoned, the circuit being completed by earthwork defences.[19] It is also possible that the earthwork defences at Verulamium[20] and Dorchester[21] were a completion of work first started in stone. Finally, at Carmarthen[22] the foundations of the wall were laid partly over a ditch associated with an earlier rampart or bank of earth, and likewise at Margidunum[23] the wall was built above an earlier defensive ditch.

Some Romano-British towns were provided with a wall and rampart from the outset: for example, Great Casterton,[24] Alchester,[25] and Caistor-by-Norwich.[26] Whether Exeter is to be placed in this category or amongst those with an independent phase of earthwork defences is uncertain. However, the slight dimensions of the bank and the absence of a turf-line on its surface shift the burden of proof onto those who would contend that the bank constituted an independent phase of the defences. The same can be said of Bath,[27] Kenchester,[28] Chichester,[29] and even Caerwent if the doubtful evidence for the existence of the palisade is disregarded;[30] at all these towns the bank stood no higher than 2m.

The wall *(Figs. 32–7)*

The wall was constructed throughout of trap which was probably quarried from Rougemont within the northern angle of the defences. Throughout its circuit the methods of its construction were generally similar. The foundations consisted of trap spalls laid in herring-bone fashion (as in the wall-core above) and bedded in clay: the depth of the foundation-trench was generally about 1.2m and its width was no greater than that of the wall at its base (see below). At the level of the contemporary ground-surface the foundations were capped by a layer of mortar, above which once again there were layers of trap spalls, pitched in herring-bone fashion although here bedded in mortar to form the core of the wall. The only exception to this method of construction was at Cricklepit Street: the foundations cut into the subsoil to a depth of 2.4m, but the upper layers of trap were mortared to a depth of 70cm below the ground surface at the rear of the wall. At this point the wall runs across a very steep slope which may account for the greater depth of its foundations.

The width of the wall at its base varies between 3.2 and 3.4m; the only exception is at Bedford Circus where its width was 2.45m, but this may result from the front of the wall having been cut back, in spite of the claim that the original facing almost certainly still survived.[31] The wall nowhere survives to its original height. The best-preserved stretch is at the South Gate where the wall is 3.5m in height; its rear is roughly faced[32] and its width is reduced from 3.4m at the base to 1.9m at the top by means of three scarcements (Fig. 35). Its full height was likely to have been about 6m with a rampart-walk and parapet above.[33] In many places the wall has clearly been refaced, and often there is a patchwork of repairs belonging to numerous periods. At several points on the circuit neat

Fig. 35: The wall of the later town immediately south-west of the South Gate.

masonry consisting of square trap blocks can be observed, and this has hitherto been taken for Roman work.[34] Excavations at Cricklepit Street have shown that the best-preserved stretch of this work in fact represents a reconstruction of the wall from foundation level between 1450 and 1550, so that doubt is cast on the antiquity of this type of facing.[35]

The gates *(Figs. 36–7)*

South Gate: the south-western tower of this gate was excavated in 1964–5 and proved to measure 5m by 5.2m.[36] The gate had been built before the wall, which abutted its north-east side. In the late fourteenth century two very large towers were built beyond the wall to create an imposing and defensible entry to the city. Stukeley[37] considered that the arch at the rear of the gate (i.e. flush with the wall) was of Roman construction; it was semi-circular and, according to Shortt, was constructed of Beer stone.[38] The overall plan of the Roman gate is uncertain, but the foundations of the wall were noted on the north-east side of South Street 11.8m from the south-west gate-tower, and thus its overall width could not have exceeded 16.8m. It was originally suggested that the gate had a single carriageway with flanking foot-passages[39] but J.S. Wacher[40] thought that the existence of a double carriageway was possible.

East Gate: nothing is known of the Roman gate, but the street-plan (Fig. 37) shows that it must have occupied roughly the same position as the medieval gate.

North Gate: the site of this gate is uncertain. No traces of it were recovered during excavation of the wall on the projected line of the *via principalis,* and it may have been sited at the head of the street leading to the market-place in front of the *forum.* Alternatively, it may lie beneath the medieval gate. If so, it would have been connected to the street-grid by a dog-leg, perhaps following the line of a road which originally led to the north-west gate (*porta principalis sinistra*) of the fortress at an oblique angle across the very steep slope.

West Gate: the street-plan (p. 69) demonstrates that this gate occupied roughly the same position as its medieval successor.

Water Gate: the southern corner of the defences crosses the base of the Coombe valley some 70m from the present north bank of the Exe. In medieval and later times the city quay was sited here and was served by the Water Gate.[41] There was probably a quay here in Roman times and the existence of a Roman predecessor of the medieval Water Gate is thus very probable.

The ditches *(Fig. 36)*

The south-east and north-east sides of the defensive circuit for the most part overlooked a tract of level land; in medieval and later times this stretch of the wall was strengthened by the addition of towers, and both the South and East Gates were of notably massive proportions. There is as yet no evidence that projecting towers were added to the defences in the fourth century as at many other Romano-British towns, but the possibility cannot be ruled out. The ditches associated with the later Roman defences have only been explored in the area beyond the South Gate; there appear to have been two separate ditch-systems, one probably contemporary with the construction of the wall and rampart, the other dating to the fourth century.

The early ditches: all traces of Roman ditches near the wall have been obliterated by the medieval ditch, itself probably recut when the City defences were refurbished during the Civil War. At Trinity Street the berm in front of these later ditches was 3.3m in width[42] and at St John's School it was 2m in width.[43] In 1976 on a site adjoining Magdalen Street, three successive ditches were sectioned at a distance of 25m from the wall. The earliest, which had a V-shaped profile, was 2.8m in depth and had been recut; its filling contained a worn *as* of Hadrian (*RIC* 673). Only one edge of the second ditch fell within the limits of the excavation, but it appeared to have been flat-bottomed. The third ditch was V-shaped and was 2m in depth. In contrast to the fourth-century ditches, which had silted up (see below), these ditches had been filled with clay and gravel containing only a little pottery, none of which need be later than the third century. The existence of another ditch much closer to the wall is very likely. At Great Casterton two ditches were associated with the early defences; one was separated from the wall by a narrow berm, the other was some 32m distant from the wall; a third possibly lay between these two.[44]

The later ditches: on the site of the Valiant Soldier public house 81m from the wall a V-shaped ditch 2m in depth was sectioned. It had been recut three times; the filling of the first recutting contained a coin

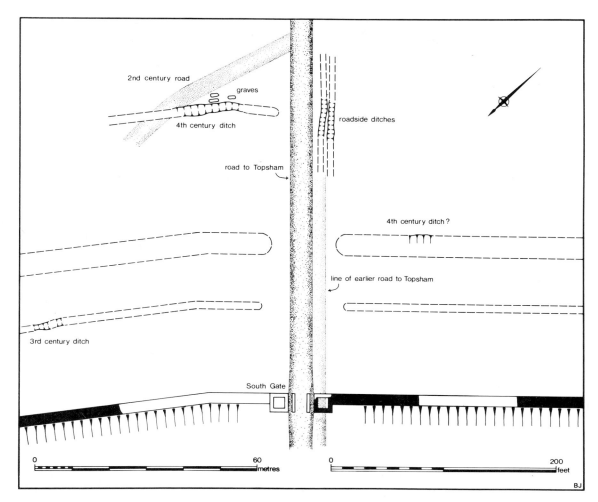

Fig. 36: Area beyond the South Gate of the defences of the later town showing ditch-systems; also roads, two of which are earlier than the defences, and late Roman graves.

of Constantine II as Caesar (330-5). The outer lip of what appeared to be a second, shallower ditch was found at a distance 44m from the wall; its filling contained a coin of Constantine II (337-41). Both ditches were filled with fine black soil mixed with small sherds of late-Roman pottery, and appeared to have silted up gradually.

There is some doubt about the function of these ditches because of their considerable distance from the wall. The outermost, although its profile certainly resembles that of a defensive ditch, may have been simply for drainage purposes, and it is not quite certain that the other was indeed a ditch. The widest ditch-system otherwise recorded from a Romano-British town is at Dorchester; this extended to a distance of 47m from the walls.[45]

Dating evidence

Establishment of the date at which the later town defences were erected is entirely dependent on pottery, particularly samian ware. Consideration must be given not only to material from the rampart, the wall and the underlying occupation-levels, but also from the ditch associated with the early defences, which presumably was filled in when the later circuit was constructed:

(i) *from occupation-levels below the rampart and wall:* at the South Gate a group of samian, 'certainly later than 150 and probably later than 160, though no certain late Antonine forms were present',[46] was found near a metal-working furnace directly beneath the rampart; the filling of a pot-hole in a street-surface under the south-west gate tower contained a *sestertius* of Hadrian which was too corroded for an assessment of its state of wear.[47] At Cricklepit Street layers below the rampart contained Hadrianic samian.

(ii) *from the filling of the ditch associated with the early defences (Fig. 9):* at Rack Street both sections across the ditch produced late Antonine samian including a stamp of *c.* 160–90. Rhenish and Nene

Valley colour-coated wares and a worn *as* of Trajan (*RIC* 653) were also found. Antonine samian was recovered from the ditch at Mermaid Yard.

(iii) *from the rampart:* Antonine samian was found in the body of the rampart at South Gate,[48] North Gate and Cricklepit Street.

(iv) *from the wall:* at Post Office Street a 'variant form 46' of late Antonine type was found at the edge of the wall footing only 1ft 3in (38cm) above the natural soil'.[49]

This material supplies a late Antonine *terminus post quem* for the construction of both the bank and the wall, which does not help in determining whether they were contemporary or the wall was a later addition to the defences. It is possible that the actual date of the new defensive circuit is somewhat later than that supplied by the pottery. The absence of black-burnished ware cooking-pots with obtuse-angled lattice, which came into production in about the mid third century, provides a *terminus ante quem,* but the difficulties of dating coarse wares in the period *c.* 200–250 are well-known; the samian ware is of little help because the importation of Central Gaulish ware ceased in *c.* 200, and East Gaulish wares, which were imported after that date, are rare at Exeter.

As already noted (p. 57), some Romano-British towns including Exeter had been provided with defences in the first century. The majority, however, were undefended until the later second century, when many, but not all, were provided with a bank or a wall and rampart. The circumstances which brought this about are thought most likely to have been the usurpation of Clodius Albinus in 193–7, and ensuing unrest.[50] But it is worth pointing out that the evidence for the date of the defences at many towns is very meagre.

NOTES

1. These are: (1) St John's School (Montgomerie-Neilson and Montague 1933–6, 57–60, 78–81). (2) Convent Garden (ibid., 65–3, 83). (3) St John's School (Ralegh Radford and Morris 1933–6, 181–7). (4) Trinity Street (Ralegh Radford and Morris 1933–6, 238–40). (5) Bishop's Palace Garden (Morris, Montague and Ralegh Radford 1937–47, 136–41). (6) Rougemont (Fox 1952, 52–3). (7) St John's School (ibid., 53–5). (8) Post Office Street (ibid., 55–6). (9) Bedford Circus (ibid., 57–9). (10) James Street (summary account: *J. Roman Stud.*, 52 (1962) 184). (11) South Gate (Fox 1968). (12) Cricklepit Street (summary account: Griffiths 1974, 169). (13) North Gate (excavations in 1978).
2. Ralegh Radford and Morris 1933–6, 181–7.
3. Fox 1952, 59, Pl. XXIII.
4. These trenches were about 8m apart.
5. Morris, Montague and Ralegh Radford 1937–47, Fig. 1.
6. Fox 1968, Fig. 5.
7. As suggested by Ralegh Radford and Morris (1933–6, 186).
8. Fox 1952, 19.
9. Boon 1969, 14.
10. Fox 1952, 59.
11. Myres, Steer and Chitty 1959, Fig. 6.
12. ibid., Fig. 13.
13. Charlesworth 1971, 163, Figs. 21 and 22.
14. Myres, Steer and Chitty 1959, Fig. 20.
15. We can safely exclude the possibility that the line of the supposed earthwork defences on this side differed from that of the wall. Section V (ibid., Fig. 3) was cut across the north-western corner of the defences and the curve described by the bank at this point establishes within rough limits the line it would have followed on the northern side of the defences.
16. Frere 1962, 119, Fig. 4.
17. Aylwin Cotton 1947, 129. It is uncertain whether these banks were equipped with additional fortifications. M. Aylwin Cotton thought that there might have been a palisade on the crest of the bank at Silchester, but that its post-holes were removed when the front of the bank was cut away to accommodate the wall. At Caerwent there was evidence which may indicate the existence of a palisade: 'The summit of the long stretch of mound exposed behind the north wall exhibited the curious feature of two irregular lines of longitudinal indents, roughly semi-circular in section, and of varying widths. They had all the appearance of being the impressions of tree trunks, and it is not unlikely that these supported a timber breastwork or stockade' (Ward 1916, 16).
18. Wacher 1961, 64; 1962, 22; 1964, 16.
19. Wacher 1974, 302.
20. Frere 1964, 108–9; Wacher 1974, 213.
21. Wacher 1974, 321.
22. ibid., 392.
23. Todd 1969, 43, Figs. 17 and 18.
24. Corder 1951, 7, Fig. 3.
25. Young 1975, 138–41, Figs. 2 and 3.
26. Wacher 1974, 234.
27. Cunliffe 1969, 166, Fig. 63.
28. Webster 1955–7, 138.
29. Holmes 1961.
30. Nash-Williams 1930, 268–9, Fig. 11. For the possible palisade see n.17 above.
31. Fox 1952, 58.
32. The rear of the wall was also roughly faced at Post Office Street: Fox 1952, 12.
33. At Caerwent the wall survives to a height of 5.2m at one point and J. Ward (1916, 12) thought that its full height must have been at least 5.5m with an 'embattled parapet' above. The wall at Silchester stands to a height of 4.5m, and an original height of 6m excluding the parapet was thought likely (Boon 1974, 100).
34. Ralegh Radford and Morris 1933–6, 183–4.
35. As noted by I. Burrow (1978, 38n. 55).
36. Fox 1968, 12–3.
37. *Itinerarium Curiosum* (1724), Iter VI, 15–6.
38. Shortt 1841, 143: 'the old South gate itself contained a circular arch of the Portland or Beer stone, supposed long anterior to the Saxon times' (Portland stone was not used at Exeter). Shortt is giving second-hand information in this passage: the gate had been demolished in 1819.
39. Fox 1968, 13.
40. Wacher 1974, 331–2.
41. Hoskins 1960, 63–4.
42. Ralegh Radford and Morris 1933–6a, 238–40.
43. Fox 1952, 53–5.
44. Corder 1954, 7; 1961, 3.
45. *RCHM Dorset II* (South-East), 548 for a nineteenth-century observation; a recent section in *Britannia* 4 (1973) 315, its position marked on Wacher 1974, 317, Fig. 70.
46. Fox 1968, 7–9.
47. ibid., 6, 14.
48. ibid., 11.
49. Fox 1952, 55–6.
50. As suggested by P. Corder (1955, 24) and followed by S.S. Frere (1978, 285–6) and J.S. Wacher (1978, 97); but G.C. Boon (1974, 66) doubts whether all second-century earth defences resulted from the usurpation of Albinus; see also the reservations expressed by M.W.C. Hassall (*Antiq. J.* 57 (1977) 128). The erection of stone defences at about this time, as at Great Casterton, Alchester and Caistor-by-Norwich (p. 62), was a very considerable undertaking, and is difficult to see as a precaution taken by Albinus when he withdrew troops from Britain to further his imperial ambitions.

VI. THE LATER TOWN

Introduction

The later second century can conveniently be taken to mark the beginning of the later period of the town. As we have seen in the preceding chapter, a new defensive circuit was erected, enclosing an area two and a half times greater than that of the early town. As a direct consequence, presumably, the street-grid was extended into the newly-enclosed areas. At about the same time alterations were made to the *basilica* and *forum* (pp. 76–9) and to the public baths.[1] Changes can also be seen in the character of the domestic occupation in the town. Throughout the greater part of the second century all the dwellings so far recorded were modest timber structures (p. 53); the earliest masonry building is on *Insula* XVIII (site 1, p. 73) and can be dated to the late second century. The change in building-techniques is illustrated well by a timber building on *Insula* IV/V (p. 69, Fig. 28, 2 and 3) to which an apse and hypocausted room, both in masonry, were added in *c.* 200. Approximately thirty masonry buildings are recorded from the later town. Many are represented solely by fragments of walls, and no complete plans have yet been recovered, but it is clear that some of the buildings (e.g. on *Insula* IV/V, p. 69) were of a considerable size. These houses were substantially built; three were equipped with mosaics, and tessellated pavements have been found in four of the remainder. Construction of buildings in timber, however, continued through the third century; at a date after *c.* 275 timber buildings were erected on the south-east side of the new street between *Insulae* XVA and XXXIII (p. 69). They were later replaced by three small stone buildings.

The results of recent excavations indicate that the later town was densely built up; only one site has failed to produce traces of buildings dating to this period.[2] This is clearly an indication of prosperity.[3] However, the most reliable guide to the quality of life in Romano-British towns must surely be the fortunes of their public buildings. Many of these buildings were excavated when archaeological techniques were at an early stage of development and little is known about their history in the fourth century. The evidence for the partial rebuilding of the *basilica* and *forum* at Exeter in the mid fourth century (pp. 76–9), including the construction of what may reasonably be interpreted as a tribunal, is of some importance because it bears witness to the continuation of civic institutions at this period.

The extension of the street-plan *(Fig. 37)*

The replacement of the early town defences by a new circuit enclosing an area two and a half times greater may have been associated with a replanning and extension of the street-plan. The only alteration to the plan within the former defences was made on the south-east side of *Insulae* XV–XIX. In the early town these *insulae* were bounded by a street which had formerly served as the *via sagularis* of the fortress. It was sectioned on the south-east side of *Insula* XIX where it had been resurfaced on at least one occasion (Fig. 27; p. 47); above the metalling a wall running from south-west to north-east was found, which probably formed part of a late Roman town-house (on *Insula* XXXIX, site 1, p. 76). The line of another street has been established only 11m to the north-west; it was sectioned on the south-east side of *Insula* XXIII at Chapel Street[4] and on the south-east side of *Insula* XVIII at Bear Street.[5] The date at which this street was laid out is uncertain, but it is likely to have superseded the street to the south-east.[6]

The extra-mural street on the north-east side of the former defences (Fig. 24; p. 55) was also built over. A layer of clay with a floor of brick-mortar which was found above the street surface may have been associated with a timber building, later replaced by a stone town-house which was probably erected between *c.* 250 and 270 (*Insula* XXII, site 1; p. 73). This street may have been replaced by another further to the north-east to form a block of five *insulae* (XX–XXIV) roughly similar in size to those within the former defensive circuit (the position of this street on Fig. 37 is conjectural). 'A clay-bound floor consisting of hard rammed gravel' was found between *Insulae* XXII and XXIII;[7] it probably represents a north-eastern extension beyond the line of the former defences of the street which ran along the south-east side of the *basilica* and *forum*. Nothing is known about the extension of the street-plan on the south-east and south-west sides of the early town, apart from a street laid out in the late third century near the southern corner (see below). If all the streets on these two sides of the early town had been extended as far as the new defensive circuit (as shown on Fig. 37), ten more *insulae* would have been created. Presumably these alterations took place shortly after the

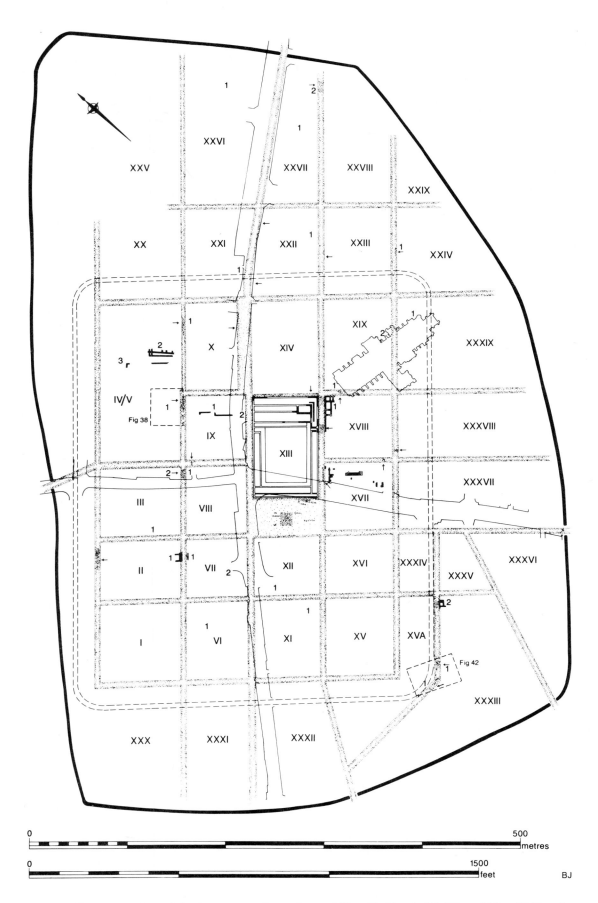

Fig. 37: The street-plan of the later town. Locations of Fig. 38 (*Insula* IV/V) and Fig. 42 (*Insulae* XVA and XXXIII) shown by broken lines. Position of sections across streets shown by arrows.

construction of the new defences at the end of the second century, although there is scarcely any dating evidence to support this notion.

A street on the south-east side of *Insulae* XV and XVI originated in the late third century.[8] It ran from south-west to north-east, presumably extending as far as the street which led from the market-place to the South Gate. Just below the crest of the steep slope above the river, the street turned through an angle of about 45° and ran towards the West Gate.

The positions of the streets leading to the North Gate and the postulated Water Gate (p. 64) are conjectural.

Gazetteer of stone buildings *(Fig. 37)*

Insula II: (1) The corner of a masonry building was recorded next to the street on the south-east side of this *insula* during building work. A corridor or veranda at the side of the street was *c.* 1.5m in width and at least 10m in length; behind it parts of two rooms were revealed, one measuring 7m by at least 4m. The walls of the building cut through the remains of five successive timber buildings (p. 53), but it was not possible to recover any dating evidence for the sequence of activity on the site.

Insula III: (1) Roman walls and a well were observed in the course of building work but no plan was recovered.[9]

(2) A wall was seen at the eastern corner of this *insula* at the side of the south-eastern street.

Insula IV/V: (1) On this site (Fig. 38), formerly divided by the street between *Insulae* IV and V (p. 47), there were two separate building plots in the late second century. The south-western plot was occupied by a rectangular building (*c.* 16.5m by *c.* 5.5m) with timber-framed walls and shallow rubble foundations (Fig. 38, 2). The boundary of this plot was marked on the north-eastern side by a ditch. At a date after *c.* 200 a masonry apse and a small room with a tile-built hypocaust were added to the south-western side of the building (Fig. 38, 3). At the same time another rectangular building of sill-beam construction was erected on the north-western side of the site, and the boundary ditch was recut and extended to the north-west. On the plot to the north-east two successive timber buildings were erected. By *c.* 270 the building on the south-west side of the site had been demolished and the site remained vacant for a while, although another ditch was dug and a fence was erected along its inner edge to mark the north-east side of the plot (Fig. 38, 4). At about the same date a substantial masonry building was erected on the north-eastern plot. It consisted of a range of three or more rooms *c.* 8m in width and at least 28m in overall length. The south-east room had a mortar floor, and the central room an earth floor over which were found two hearths and an oven. The open areas to the south-west and north-east were metalled. At a later date a veranda or corridor *c.* 2.3m in width was added to the north-east side of the range. Two rooms measuring *c.* 3.8m by *c.* 3.3m and *c.* 9.5m by *c.* 2.7m were built on the south-west side of the range in the second quarter of the fourth century. The smaller room was equipped with a hypocaust, the piers of which were constructed of mortared rubble; its stokehole opened into the larger room (Fig. 39).

Stukeley records the discovery of 'a great Roman pavement of little white square stones' in Pancras Lane. In 1887 two further fragments of a white tessellated pavement or pavements were found on either side of Pancras Lane.[10] All these fragments were perhaps from the same pavement; the position of those found in 1887 can be fixed some 5–10m north-east of the excavated range. In 1887 a fragment of mosaic was also found north-east of Pancras Lane; a coloured drawing (Fig. 40) made at the time of discovery shows that the fragment measured 3.22m by 1.93m and that it consisted of a patterned band of intersecting circles between plain borders.[11] It seems very likely that these two pavements belonged to a range of rooms alongside the street, which formed part of the building excavated to the south-west. On the south-west side of site 2 on this *insula* (see below) a wall was found running from north-west to south-east at a distance of 34m from the range on site 1; this wall may have been an extension of another wall occupying the same line on site 3, which turned a corner to the south-west. If these walls and the excavated range all belonged to the same building, its overall dimensions would have been 42m from south-west to north-east and 56m from north-west to south-east.

On site 1 the area south-west of the range was resurfaced after 326, the date of a coin from the metalling. A tank was dug next to the room with the hypocaust, and was supplied with water by a pipe which led from the street (Fig. 38, 5). A deposit of brown soil containing coins going down to 367–75 had accumulated over the metalling; cobbles had been embedded in the soil around the tank. It may well be that this area was used as a stockyard which was provided with facilities for watering

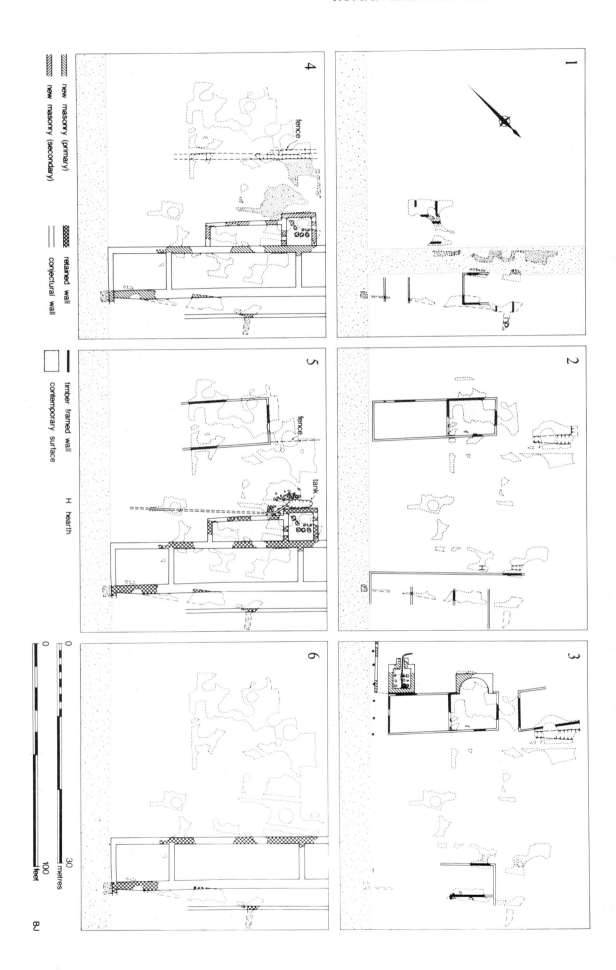

Fig. 38: Successive buildings on *Insula* IV/V: (1) Early second century (p. 53) (2) Late second century (3) *c.* 200 (4) *c.* 270 with additions after 326 (5) Mid fourth century (6) After *c.* 370.

Fig. 39:Insula IV/V, site 1. View from the north-west of the two rooms added to the north-east side of the masonry building, see Fig. 38, 4. The vertical 2m scale stands next to one of the rubble-built masonry supports of the hypocaust; to the left can be seen the north-east side of the furnace arch. Most of the Roman walls are reduced to foundation level or have been entirely robbed, and the Roman levels have been removed in many places by medieval pits.

animals; probable stock enclosures have been found on the north-west side of this *insula* (site 3). After the first quarter of the fourth century a timber building (6.5m by at least 10.5m) supported on dwarf walls was erected on the south-west plot and the boundary fence was replaced. After *c.* 370 both plots were cleared of all buildings except the range of three rooms on the north-east side (Fig. 38, 6). The latter were demolished or fell into decay at an unknown date and the whole site was then covered by an accumulation of post-Roman dark soil.

(2) On the south-west side of the site a stone wall at least 6m in length was found which may have formed the north-east wall of the building explored on site 1 (see above). The north-east side of the site was occupied by a building represented by a range of at least five rooms with an overall length of between 34m and 48m. Two of the rooms were provided with hypocausts; one, in the room at the north-west end of the range, was a later insertion and was of *pila*-type. The second hypocaust, in the room at the centre of the excavated portion of the range, was channelled and may have belonged to

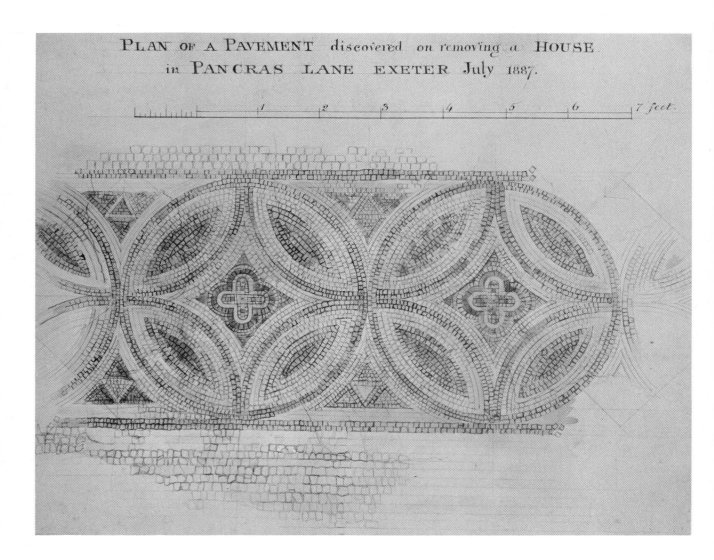

PLAN OF A PAVEMENT discovered on removing a HOUSE
in PANCRAS LANE EXETER July 1887.

Fig. 40: Drawing of a mosaic discovered just to the north-east of *Insula* IV/V site 1, in 1887. Reproduced by permission of the Devon and Exeter Institution.

the original construction of the building; fragments of a red tessellated pavement were found in the debris filling the hypocaust. On the south-west side of the range there was a corridor at least 21.7m in length with a small room at the north-west end.

(3) The northern corner of a masonry building fell just within the limits of excavation on the south-east side of the site; as noted above, it may have formed part of the building explored on site 1. Otherwise, later Roman occupation on this site, which extended to within 10m of the street on the north-west side of the *insula,* was represented by a series of successive ditches forming irregular enclosures. The latest ditches were filled after the middle of the fourth century; one contained a marble head (p. 81; Fig. 48). It is possible that these enclosures were used as pounds for cattle; a deposit of cow skulls was found in one ditch.

Insula VI: (1) In 1812 a tessellated pavement was found in digging the foundations of the new chapel at the Mint.[12] In 1837 labourers laying gas-pipes in the Mint (presumably in the alley itself) came upon a Roman foundation with a coin of Faustina II embedded in it.[13]

Insula VII: (1) A wall was traced along the side of the street on the north-west side of the *insula.* It was directly opposite the building on *Insula* II, site 1, with which its construction was contemporary.

(2) A wall 90cm in width was found running from south-west to north-east.[14]

Insula VIII: (1) The corner of a masonry building was found in 1974 at the junction of the streets on the north-west and north-east sides of this *insula.*

Insula IX: (1) The remains of a building of later second- or early third-century date were excavated in 1973; its foundations, of trap rubble bonded with clay, probably supported a timber superstructure. Above this structure was found the north-west corner of a masonry building with walls *c*. 60cm in width, which was erected after *c*. 270; over the original gravel floor within the angle of the walls there was a tessellated pavement.[15] Under the pavement outside the modern tenement (197 High Street) two more fragments of tessellation were found;[16] they may belong to the building excavated to the north-west.

(2) A wall was revealed in a section next to the street on the south-east side of the *insula;*[17] it may have formed part of the building on site 1.

Insula X: (1) Timber buildings on this site were demolished in the first half of the second century (p. 55) and the site remained vacant until after *c*. 250. When construction of a masonry building commenced, the site was used as a builders' yard. The lowest levels consisted of spreads of mortar, suggesting that the yard was used at first for mortar-mixing. Above were deposits consisting of spalls of Purbeck marble and fine-grained sandstone; in one area a heap of white lias chips must have resulted from the preparation of *tesserae,* and elsewhere there was evidence for the working of roof-slates. These deposits were cut by a wall which was constructed alongside the street and were sealed by the rough cobbling of a courtyard. The structure with which the builders' yard was associated may have been situated just to the north-east where in 1843 and 1845 part of a hypocaust, foundations and 'the remains of Roman zig-zag or herring-bone pebble pavements' came to light.[18]

Insula XI: (1) A room measuring 4.2m by 3.2m with walls still standing to a height of 1.2m was excavated on this site; it was thought to have been equipped with a hypocaust. Nearby was found a short length of wall.[19]

Insula XII: (1) An unpublished account of observations made by Col. Ransom Pickard on this site during building-work is lodged in Rougemont House Museum: it was originally accompanied by plans and photographs which unfortunately have been lost. It was claimed that a number of walls were of Roman construction, although underpinned and reused in medieval times; but this was founded on a belief that trap, from which the walls were built, was not used for domestic building in medieval Exeter, which is quite untrue. However, R.G. Goodchild,[20] who must have seen the lost plans and photographs, considered that one wall, 9.2m in length and 60cm in width, was certainly Roman.

Insula XVA: (1) Opposite the three stone buildings on *Insula* XXXIII, site 1, a stone building was excavated with a frontage onto the street *c*. 12.5m in width; it was built in the middle of the fourth century (Fig. 42).

Insula XVIII: (1) The remains of two successive masonry buildings were excavated on a site at the northern corner of the *insula.*[21] The earlier building consisted of an L-shaped range of at least five rooms with walls 55cm in width; it appeared to be of late second-century date. Before *c*. 250 it was substantially rebuilt, although the north-east range of the earlier building may well have been retained. One room contained a badly damaged mosaic; a border of coarse red *tesserae* enclosed a guilloche and a square or rectangular pattern. The date at which the building fell into decay or was demolished is unknown.

Insula XIX: (1) Two successive mortar floors on pitched rubble foundations may have been associated with either a late Roman building or a Saxon church.[22] (2) Part of a room with an apse and a channelled hypocaust was excavated.[23]

Insula XXI: (1) In 1975 a wall *c*. 60cm in width was exposed when the cellar-walls of 228 High Street were removed; it was associated with a number of floor-levels and appeared to have been partly rebuilt.

Insula XXII: (1) Above an earlier street which had run from north-west to south-east (p. 55) there was a layer of clay with a floor of brick-mortar over it.[24] This may represent the remains of a building, perhaps of timber, which was erected when the street went out of use, presumably at the end of the second century. The site was then covered with a deposit of dark soil *c*. 65cm in depth, and a masonry building with three or more rooms was erected.[25] Fragments of mosaic pavements were found in two of the rooms and in the third an area of coarse red *tesserae* may have formed the border of another mosaic. Room 1 measured 5.65m from north-west to south-east and at least 5.8m from north-east to south-west; the mosaic, which was poorly preserved, had a border of coarse red *tesserae*

Fig. 41: Insula XXXIII, site 1. Circular oven with a plank-lined ash pit in front of it; found inside a late third-century timber building. 1m scale.

enclosing a key-pattern and a guilloche of four strands. Room 2 was 2.15m in width and had a mosaic with a key-pattern. Medieval debris was found immediately above the floors and the date at which the building fell into decay or was demolished is unknown.

Insula XXIV: (1) Part of a building was excavated on the south-east side of a street which was probably laid out in the late second century (p. 67). The corner of a single room measuring 5.2m by 4.5m was explored;[26] its interior was occupied by drains and hearths. Very little material was associated with its construction but it is unlikely to have been erected before the street was laid out; it appeared to have been demolished at the beginning of the fourth century.

Insula XXVI: (1) Shortt[27] noted 'a solid foundation of Roman masonry, of the usual materials'.

Insula XXVII: (1) Fragmentary foundations were found on two slightly different alignments.[28] (2) A short length of foundation was found on the north-east side of the street.[29]

Insula XXXIII: (1) This site was occupied by one or more timber buildings (Fig. 42) which probably date from after *c.* 275 when the street on the north-west side of this *insula* was first laid out (p. 69). The building or buildings were rebuilt in timber, and one room (below the later stone building with ovens) contained two circular ovens, one with a plank-lined ash pit with a partly tiled floor in front of it (Fig. 41) and the other formed by a large storage jar laid on its side. The building or buildings were destroyed by fire and were replaced by three separate stone structures. Only one wall of the building on the north-east side of the site fell within the limits of the excavation; it was separated from its neighbour to the south-west by a passage 2m in width which had a metalled

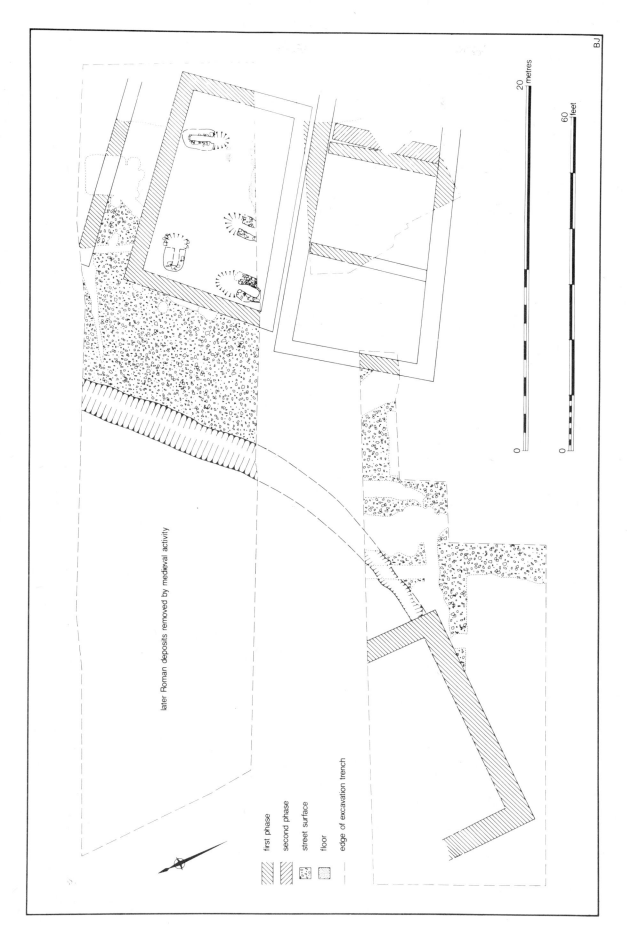

later Roman deposits removed by medieval activity

first phase
second phase
street surface
floor
edge of excavation trench

metres 20

feet 60

0

0

BJ

Fig. 42: Masonry buildings on *Insulae* XVA and XXXIII. The building which contains four ovens dates from the second quarter of the fourth century. For the location of this plan, see Fig. 37.

surface. The building to the south-west of the passage measured 8m by 12m and from its wall-foundations there came a coin of 330–5. The interior of the building contained four substantially-constructed ovens. To the south-west there was another masonry building measuring 8m by at least 13m; it was divided into two or more rooms; its end wall had been rebuilt. The demolition or decay of these buildings was represented by a layer of rubble and slates along the south-east side of the adjoining street.

(2) About 55m north-east of the buildings just described the remains of two successive buildings were found on the frontage of the street. The first building was of timber construction and probably dates from *c.* 275 when the street was laid out (p. 69). Its successor was constructed in stone and appeared to consist of a range of at least three small rooms. A coin of 346–50 was found in the debris resulting from demolition or decay above the floor-levels of the building.

Insula XXXIX: (1) Three Roman walls were found running parallel to each other from south-west to north-east;[30] that to the north-west was built above a street which probably remained in use until the end of the second century (p. 47). In the vicinity of this site a tessellated pavement was found in 1843; it measured *c.* 7m from north-east to south-east and was *c.* 2.4m in width. The pavement was 'composed of small cubes or quadrangular pieces of tile intersected by others of a species of common black river pebble. Some of the little fragments are larger than others so as to take a deeper hold of the bed of cement which serves as a base and thus form a sort of binding course to give stability to the whole'.[31] The tessellated pavement and the walls probably belonged to the same building.

The *basilica* and *forum* (Figs. 43 and 45)

No alterations were made to the *basilica* and *forum* until the late Antonine period, when some parts of the building were replanned (Fig. 43).[32] There are no signs that the rebuilding took place because of a deterioration in the fabric.

The *basilica* and range of rooms on its north-east side were not affected by the building-work, although a new surface had been laid at a higher level in the *forum*-courtyard. The south-east *forum*-portico was demolished and replaced by a substantial wall which also cut across the south-east end of the passage or aisle in front of the *basilica*. Both ends of the passage leading from the street to the portico were walled up, and the entry of the room on the south-west side of the passage was also blocked. On the south-east side of the *basilica* the narrow passage and the room at its south-west end remained in use. The courtyard, however, was roofed over and divided into two or more rooms by wooden partitions. The north-easternmost room, which measured 4.9m by 6m, was divided into two parts by another wooden partition; the end of the north-west part was screened off, perhaps to form a large cupboard. The adjacent room was entered from the narrow passage through a door which had been cut through the north-west wall; its position was marked by a large stone threshold block. The passage on the north-east side of the *basilica* remained in use, although its level was raised. Before the next phase of alterations, but at some date after the work described above was carried out, the courtyard on the north-east side of the passage was roofed over and apparently divided into shops which opened onto the narrow street or lane on the north-east side of the *insula*.[33]

At a date in the last quarter of the third century, or perhaps a little later, parts of the *basilica* and *forum* were rebuilt.[34] The level of the floor in the aisle or passage along the front of the *basilica* was raised by up to 45cm, burying the steps which had led up to the *basilica*. The south-west wall of the aisle or passage was replaced by what may have been a stylobate. The *forum*-courtyard was also resurfaced and the wall of the room on its south-east side was rebuilt. Alterations were also made to the range on the south-east side of the *basilica*. A channelled hypocaust was inserted in the room at the south-west end; at the north-east end of the range the wooden partitions were removed. The adjacent street, was covered by a thick layer of broken roof-tiles mixed with wall-plaster, some fragments of which were covered with doodles including the letters *k*, *d* and ...*e canem* ..., probably for *cave canem* ('beware of the dog'), and also a sketch of a 'pin man'.[35] This material had probably been stripped from the range of rooms to the north-west, which was re-roofed in Devon slate. The shop at the eastern corner of the *insula* appears to have caught fire, perhaps while rebuilding was in progress; its floor was covered with charcoal and burnt tile fragments.

In the middle of the fourth century the *basilica* and *forum* once more underwent considerable replanning (Fig. 44).[36] The *basilica* was extended at its south-east end across the site of the range of rooms adjacent to the street. A few courses of the former end-wall of the *basilica* may have been left in

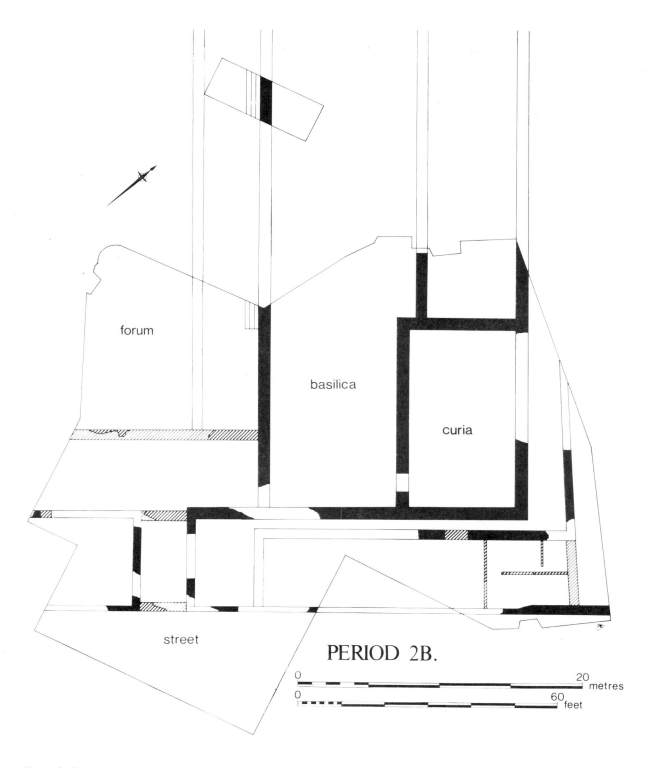

Fig. 43: Eastern corner of the *basilica* and *forum* showing alterations carried out at the end of the second century. Walls in black retained from the original phase of construction in *c.* 80 (see Fig. 29).

position to retain a raised floor on its south-east side, thus forming a platform which may have served as a tribunal; a shallow foundation which crossed the *basilica* 2m to the north-west may have supported a row of columns or balustrade separating the possible tribunal from the rest of the hall. The room which has been identified as the *curia* was also extended as far as the street; its size was now 15m by 7.6m. A wall built across its north-west end divided off a room measuring 4m by 7.6m.

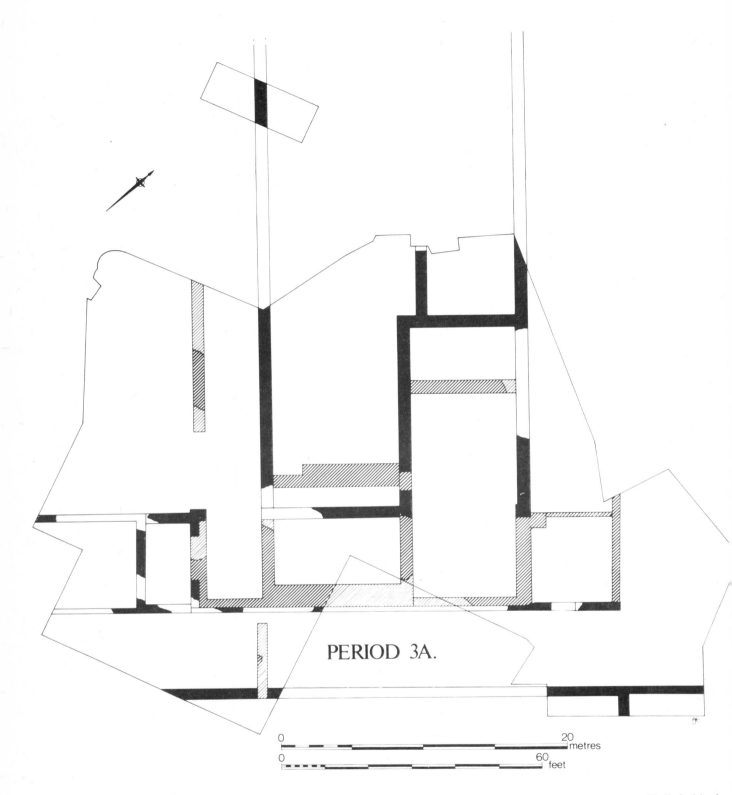

PERIOD 3A.

0 _____ 20
                                    metres
0 _____ 60
                                    feet

Fig. 44: Eastern corner of the *basilica* and *forum* showing alterations carried out in the mid fourth century. Walls in black retained from previous phases of construction (see Figs. 25 and 43).

Whether the larger of these two rooms still served as the *curia* is uncertain; if it did, the smaller room may have been used to house archives. The aisle or portico on the south-west side of the *basilica* was reduced to ground level and another wall was built re-using the old foundations; it was also extended across the site of the room with a channelled hypocaust (see above). The range of rooms south-east of the *forum*-courtyard may have remained in use, although the room which had occupied the site of the original south-east *forum*-portico seems to have been demolished. On the north-east side of the *basilica* the range of shops was demolished and a narrower range was erected, its south-west wall formed by the side wall of the *basilica*. The line of the path or lane next to the range was shifted *c.* 2.5m to the south-west, covering the former north-east wall of the range. A wall was found cutting across the street on the south-east side of the *basilica* and *forum;* it may have been associated with the building-work in the late third century, but, equally, may be associated with the mid fourth-century work.

NOTES

1. Walls on the north-west and south-east sides of the baths *insula* appear to have been constructed in the later second century (*EAR* (i), 122).
2. *Insula* I, on a small site near the centre of the *insula*. Most of *Insula* IV/V, site 3 (p. 72) was occupied by ditched enclosures, although the corner of a building fell just within the limits of the excavation.
3. J.S. Wacher (1974, 333), writing of the domestic occupation in the later town, judged that 'the general standard was not very good, and the fact that so few tessellated or mosaic pavements have been recorded from Exeter is a measure of either the comparative poverty of the inhabitants or their lack of *aemulatio'*. At first sight this is a compelling view; the *civitas* capitals at Dorchester and Cirencester, for example, have each produced dozens of mosaics. Exeter, however, unlike the small medieval towns at Dorchester and Cirencester, was intensively occupied from the tenth or eleventh centuries, and by the seventeenth and eighteenth centuries, when the discovery of mosaics was likely to have been recorded, large areas of the later Roman deposits had been removed. This is likely to account for the poor showing at Exeter.
4. Greenfield 1964, 342, Fig. 5: 'a single layer of broken trap rock with a gully along its south-east side'.
5. Fox 1952, 4, Pl. VIII.
6. The street may have been moved to the north-west because the site of the demolished rampart and filled ditch on its south-east side was unsuitable for building-plots. At Mermaid Yard (Fig. 9) the rampart was still 90cm high after its demolition and a section across the ditch at Rack Street showed that its late Antonine filling had subsided gradually over a period of about a century.
7. At the Annuellars' College in 1933 (Montgomerie-Neilson and Montague 1933–6, 81).
8. The original metalling of the street was later than a deposit containing a scattered hoard of 25 or 26 coins which was put together in *c.* 275 (Shiel 1978, 256–8, Hoard B).
9. Montgomerie-Neilson and Montague 1933–6, 128–30.
10. References collected by R.G. Goodchild in Fox 1952, 99–100.
11. The coloured drawing, hitherto unpublished, is in the possession of the Devon and Exeter Institution. D.J. Smith, who examined a photograph and colour transparency of the drawing, commented that there were no significant parallels to the mosaic, although bands of intersecting circles are known elsewhere and are often used for the floors of corridors.
12. Thomas 1875, 34.
13. Shortt 1840, 55.
14. Montgomerie-Neilson and Montague 1933–6, 128–30.
15. This may be the pavement recorded by Dean Milles (1782, 1).
16. One was of square brick *tesserae;* the other, a section of which is in Rougemont House Museum, consisted of fragments of roofing *tegulae* laid on edge and interspersed with squares of grey and white *tesserae (Woolmer's Exeter and Plymouth Gazette, June 3 and 6, 1874).*
17. *EAR* (i), 121, Fig. 41, Sect. 33.
18. References collected by R.G. Goodchild in Fox 1952, 99.
19. Montgomerie-Neilson and Montague 1933–6, 124–8.
20. In Fox 1952, 100–1.
21. *EAR* (i), 116–8.
22. ibid., 118.
23. Morris 1933–6, 227–8.
24. Fox 1952, Pl. XXVI, Sect. A–B.
25. Fox 1952, 47–9. Examination of pottery from levels below the building (particularly ibid., Fig. 18, 58–9) suggests a construction-date in the second half of the third century rather than *c.* 200 as originally proposed.
26. Greenfield 1964.
27. Shortt 1840, 55.
28. Fox 1952, 49–50, Pl XIXA.
29. ibid., 51–2, Pls. XIXD, XXIV.
30. Morris 1933–6, 228–31.
31. W.T.P. Shortt in *Woolmer's Exeter and Plymouth Gazette,* January 7, 1843.
32. *EAR* (i), 91–6.
33. ibid., 97.
34. ibid., 98–102.
35. M.W.C. Hassall in ibid., 243, Fig. 77.
36. ibid., 104–9.

VII. ASPECTS OF SOCIAL AND ECONOMIC LIFE

Introduction

Economic activities within the town have left a very partial record and in this chapter it is only possible to refer to topics such as animal husbandry and pottery production and importation. Scarcely anything is known about manufacturing processes in the town. A small series of objects with religious associations helps to compensate for the failure to discover any temple-sites and our ignorance of the extent of the cemeteries and the burial-rites practised in them.

Industries and trade

The majority of the population must have depended, directly or indirectly, on agriculture for its livelihood (for the evidence of animal husbandry, see p. 81). A possible stock-yard and stock-enclosures have been recognised within the town on *Insula* IV/V (sites 1 and 3, pp. 69, 72). Some evidence for other industries has been recovered. Slags from the working of bronze and iron are found in levels of all periods, likewise crucibles containing residues of bronze. A metal-working hearth near the later Roman South Gate was probably for the cupellation of silver from lead or copper alloys; it was dated to the mid second century.[1] In addition to the evidence of metal-working, off-cuts attest the manufacture of shale and bone objects within the town. Many masons are likely to have been employed within the later town, to judge from the number and extent of the stone buildings. Other trades regrettably have left little trace, but of the existence of carpenters, tanners and other workers and dealers in perishable goods, there can be no doubt.

As far as is known, very little pottery was produced in the vicinity of Exeter after the beginning of the second century. A minor industry which operated in the second and third centuries produced wheel-thrown copies of black-burnished ware forms.[2] Some second-century mortaria appear to be local, but throughout the second century and through much of the third the majority of mortaria were imported from other parts of Britain and the Continent (see below). The principal source of pottery was the black-burnished ware industry of south-east Dorset, although in the later first and second centuries appreciable quantities were supplied from elsewhere, notably products in a micaceous grey fabric.[3] By the late third century, however, black-burnished wares took up 90% of the market; most of the remaining pottery was supplied by an industry in south Devon.

From the late first century onwards pottery imported from the Continent decreased both in quantity and in the diversity of its sources. Soon after the beginning of the second century Central Gaul replaced South Gaul as the source of samian ware. Importation of samian continued down to the early third century. Until the Antonine period the importation of other fine wares was confined mostly to colour-coated beakers from Central Gaul. In the later second century fine wares were imported from the Mosel and the Rhineland areas, and colour-coated vessels also reached Exeter from the Nene valley. Towards the end of the third century the Oxford and New Forest industries took a predominant place in the supply of fine wares. In the fourth century the only continental fine wares of any importance were vessels in *céramique à l'éponge* from Aquitania.

For the supply of mortaria the town relied for the most part on imports from southern England and the Continent.[4] In the second century there are numerous mortaria from southern England, including examples almost certainly from Shepton Mallet in Somerset, and from Gaul; after the middle of the second century mortaria which were probably the products of an industry in the Rhineland are common. In the later third and fourth centuries mortaria were imported from the Oxford region. The importation of amphorae continued after the departure of the legion in *c.* 75; the principal source until the mid third century was Spain, but in levels dating to the second half of the fourth century considerable numbers of amphorae from North Africa and elsewhere in the Mediterranean are found.

Also worthy of comment are the trade contacts of Exeter with south Devon and Cornwall. In the first century pottery produced at Exeter appears in the forts at Okehampton and Nanstallon, and at the civil site at Carvossa, Probus (p. 41). A small amount of pottery reached Exeter from south Devon and Cornwall in the first and second centuries. From the beginning of the third century the importation of pottery from south Devon increased steadily until in the late third century it comprised about 10% of most large pottery assemblages. Pottery from south Devon has also been recovered from the villas at Holcombe and Seaton, and at a site near Taunton.[5] At the end of the second century Devon slate from the vicinity of Ashburton began to be used for roofing at Exeter; it has also been found on villa-sites in Somerset.[6] Stone bowls in elvan and greisen from Cornwall also found their way to Exeter in the third and fourth centuries. Thus the distribution of these three types of material suggests that after *c.* 200 trade between Exeter and areas to the west increased to a considerable degree.

Diet and animal husbandry

Evidence for the diet of the population at Exeter is almost entirely confined to animal bones; these have recently been the subject of a comprehensive study by M. Maltby.[7] Throughout the Roman period cattle were of the greatest importance as a source of meat. Most were as least four and a half years old when slaughtered, which suggests they were used as draught animals and as a source of dairy products; otherwise it would have been uneconomical to have kept them until this age. There are signs that in the fourth century the exploitation of cattle as a source of meat increased; the bones of immature animals are more common at this period.[8] Pigs, sheep and goats also played a part in the diet of the inhabitants. Many pigs were killed during the first year of life and sucking-pig may have been a popular dish. Sheep appear to have been more numerous than goats and, of course, supplied wool as well as meat. The bones of horses, dogs and cats are much rarer. Game was rarely eaten, although the bones of red and roe deer occur in Roman levels at Exeter more frequently than in medieval layers. Other wild animals are represented by the bones of three foxes, a badger and an otter.

Domestic fowl also provided meat, as did the grey-lag or domestic goose, the mallard or domestic duck, woodcock, pigeon, teal, partridge and stock-dove, although these latter were of little importance. From a deposit of late first-century date were recovered the remains of a common crane. a bird no longer found in the British Isles. The bones of other birds which were probably not eaten have also been found. Most common are those of ravens; they were probably scavengers although some may have been tamed as pets.

Fish-bones are comparatively rare in Roman deposits and it seems likely that they were less important as food items than in the medieval period.[9] Hake was most common but conger eel, whiting, cod or pollack, sea bream, gurnard, wrass, turbot, salmon and bream were also eaten. Shell-fish were probably eaten more frequently; oyster-shells are very common finds.[10]

The virtual absence of water-logged Roman deposits means that little has been learnt about other food-stuffs. A stone-lined well on *Insula* X (site 2, p. 55) contained a wide range of organic remains; hazel-nuts and plum-stones were easily recognizable.

Religious life *(Figs. 45–9)*

No temples or religious sites, apart from cemeteries (pp. 41–4), are known at Exeter. However, a number of objects with religious associations have come to light:

(i) *Pipe-clay statuettes:* a statuette of Venus (Fig. 45) was found in a plank-lined tank at the northern corner of *Insula* VIII (site 1, p. 72); it was associated with pottery of late second-century date. A statuette of *Dea Nutrix* was recovered during building-work at the western corner of *Insula* XIV (Fig. 46)[11] and the neck from the model of a bird, probably a cock, came from a mid second-century deposit on *Insula* IV/V (site 1, p. 53).

(ii) *Bronze statuettes:* in July 1778 six statuettes were found together on the south-east side of *Insula* IX (Fig. 47).[12] They portray Mercury (two examples), Apollo, Mars, Fortuna and a small cock; two bronze pedestals, one square and one circular, were also found. The present whereabouts of these objects is not known. In December 1836 a statuette *c.* 7.5cm in height was found 'in removing some old walls' in the West Quarter (i.e. in the southern quadrant of the town between Fore Street and South Street).[13] It was said to portray Julius Caesar and the description is certainly that of a figure in military dress.[14]

(iii) *Marble head* (Fig. 48): this was recovered from a fourth-century enclosure ditch on *Insula* IV/V (site 3, p. 72) amidst rubble which may have come from the building to the south-east. J. M. C. Toynbee, however, believes that this piece belongs to the latter part of the first century;[15] it is sculptured in the realistic style typical of the Flavian period and some use has been made of the drill, which was coming into fashion at that time. The head is that of an elderly man; it has been worked in

Fig. 45: Pipe-clay statuette of Venus from *Insula* VIII. Height 134mm.

Fig. 46: Pipe-clay statuette of *Dea Nutrix* from *Insula* XIV. Height 112mm.

Fig. 47: Bronze statuettes from *Insulae* IX, found in 1778. They portray Fortuna (Fig. 1), Mercury (Figs. 2 and 3), Mars (Fig. 4), Apollo (Fig. 5) and a bronze cock. Reproduced from *Archaeologia,* vol. vi.

imported marble by a Mediterranean sculptor. Its small size suggests that it was an *imago* or memorial bust which may have been placed in the shrine of a private house.

(iv) *Phalli:* two sculptures of *phalli* are known from the town; they were probably fixed to the exterior of buildings where their function was to ward off the evil eye. One was found on the south-east side of the *basilica* in a late Antonine context;[16] the other was found on *Insula* IV/V (site 3, p. 72) in a deposit of fourth-century date.

(v) *Fragment of a faience model of a sistrum* (Fig. 49): this fragment from a model of a *sistrum* (a rattle used in religious ceremonies) was found in 1833 in South Street at Bel or Bull Hill 'in digging under Mr. Godolphins's late premises . . . behind the Deanery', a tenement in the north-west part of South Street on its north-east side, i.e. on *Insula* XVIII which was the site of the public baths (p. 52).[17] The model found its way into the hands of a Mr. Ross and eventually into the collection of the Rougemont House Museum. It is one of the few relics which may possibly be associated with the worship of Isis in Britain, but, although recent writers have not questioned its authenticity,[18] regrettably there are good reasons for doing so. M. G. Williams[19] has described the model as follows: 'Mask of Isis as Hathor, goddess of music and dancing. Part of a model of a *sistrum*, Egyptian faience, 7.5cm by 7.5cm. XXVIth dynasty, royal title on each side, but only the uppermost hieroglyph survives. Dated to *c.* 580 B.C., the reign of Haa-ab-aa, Uah-ab-Ra, Apries, Pharoah Hophra. From royal tomb at Saïs, when capital of Egypt; found by tomb robbers, temp.?; mutilated, glaze fractured . . .'. Then follow speculations about how the model may have passed from hand to hand, eventually reaching Exeter when it was already 600 years old. But the presence of the model at

Penates found at Exeter.

Fig. 47

Fig. 48: Marble head of late first-century date found in a ditch on *Insula* IV/V, site 3. Height 65mm.

Fig. 49: Fragment of a faience model of a *sistrum* (rattle) from South Street. Egyptian, sixth century B.C. Height 71mm.

Exeter can be accounted for in another way: as in the case of the Greek Imperial and Byzantine coins (p. 87 n.6), Shortt or the person who communicated the 'discovery' to him may have been given material from a private collection passed off as a genuine site-find (p. 2).

(vi) *A chi-rho symbol:* a sherd of pottery with a *chi-rho* symbol scratched on it was found in post-Roman dark soil above the metalling of the market-place on the south-west side of the *forum* (p. 52).[20] The sherd is from the shoulder of a black-burnished ware cooking-pot;[21] the interior displays the 'fettling' marks which are usually found on these vessels in the later Roman period.[22] The form taken by the *chi-rho* symbol, where one arm of the *chi* is missing, dates from the middle of the fourth century.[23]

NOTES

1. Fox 1968, 7–9.
2. *EAR* (i), 192–3 (fabric *101*); for the pottery from Exeter see *EAR* (iv) forthcoming.
3. *EAR* (i), 193 (fabric *125*).
4. Information from K. Hartley: see *EAR* (i), 195–221 (*passim*); *EAR* (iv) forthcoming.
5. Holcombe, unpublished; Seaton, unpublished (information from R. J. Silvester); Taunton, unpublished (information from M. Langdon). There are also about thirty vessels in this highly distinctive fabric from recent excavations at London; I am grateful to B. Richardson for showing me this material.
6. Williams 1971, 105–7.
7. *EAR* (ii) of which this section is a brief summary which can scarcely do justice to the subject.
8. For a possible stockyard and stock-enclosure on *Insulae* IV/V, sites 1 and 3, see pp. 69, 72.
9. See M. Wilkinson in *EAR* (ii), 74–81.
10. Molluscan shells have yet to receive detailed study but the shells of whelks and mussels have also been recognized.
11. *J. Roman Stud.*, 15 (1925) 237; the Exeter statuette and similar examples are discussed by F. Jenkins in Todd 1969, 93–5.
12. Milles 1782; for excavations in the tenement under which they were found see *EAR* (i), 60, 120–1.
13. The statuette is in the British Museum, reference number 38, 9–6, 1 (information in a letter from T. D. Kendrick to R. G. Goodchild in October 1933) but a recent search failed to locate it.
14. Shortt 1840, 143.
15. In a letter to J. Collis in 1971.
16. *EAR* (i), 146, Fig. 49, 9.
17. Shortt 1840, 29, 140; 1841, 70–1, Pl. IV where the drawing is rather inaccurate, especially with regard to the hieroglyphs within the cartouche.
18. Harris and Harris 1965, 90; Green 1976, 199. These authors list the evidence for the veneration of Isis in Britain (respectively pp. 74–95 and p. 58); to their list can now be added an altar from London which mentions the restoration of a temple of Isis (*Britannia*, 7 (1976) 378–9).
19. Williams 1940, 4 and in typewritten notes attached to an off-print of her article lodged in the Rougemont House Museum.
20. Fox 1952, 92.
21. It is in fabric *31* (*EAR (i)*, 193).
22. Farrar 1973, 76.
23. Fox 1952, 92.

EPILOGUE: THE END OF THE ROMAN TOWN

The fourth century in Britain, although in general a period of prosperity, saw a mounting threat from external enemies who also menaced the rest of the Western Roman Empire. By the end of the century most of the Roman garrisons had been withdrawn from Britain, either by usurpers attempting to gain control of the Western Provinces, or by the legitimate emperor in order to defend Gaul and Italy against barbarian attacks. In 410 the towns of Britain were obliged to organize their own defence against Saxon raids; the Roman administration, powerless to defend the province, was expelled. Britain was no longer part of the Roman Empire. The decline of Romano-British civilisation which followed these events was rapid. By the end of the fourth century little fresh coinage was reaching Britain and the coins then in use had probably ceased to circulate by c. 430. The latest reliably attested Roman coin at Exeter is of the House of Theodosius (an issue dated to 388–92). Soon after the beginning of the fifth century the important centres of pottery production (p. 80) which supplied Exeter went out of operation; furthermore, it is difficult to draw distinctions between pottery of mid and late fourth-century date. Thus the two principal means of dating archaeological deposits, coins and pottery, fail us before the end of the fourth century. In addition many late Roman deposits at Exeter have been removed by medieval and later activities. These circumstances make it impossible to chart the decline of the Roman town.

The only event of significance which can be given an approximate date is the demolition of the *forum* and *basilica,* and this can only be established within broad limits.[1] No further alterations were made to the buildings after the extensive alterations which took place in the mid fourth century (pp. 76–9), but the laying of a new floor in the *basilica,* the make-up for which contained a well-circulated coin of Valens (364–78), suggests nevertheless that the buildings remained in use for some time. Their demolition took place before a cemetery was established on the site in about the middle of the fifth century (see below). There were clear signs that the debris from the demolition had been removed from the site: the fills of early post-Roman features were for the most part free of building rubble, and only two pieces of architectural stonework from the *basilica* and *forum* were recovered from post-Roman deposits. The demolition of these buildings can be taken to mark the end of civic institutions at Exeter, although not, perhaps, the end of organised life within the town, for the work of demolition and clearance of the site must have been a very considerable undertaking.

A number of pits dug through the later Roman levels can be attributed to a period of activity between the demolition of the *basilica* and *forum* and the establishment of a cemetery on the site. Most were of a small size and their purpose is uncertain. One of the pits, however, which was dug through the floor of the room identified as the *curia,* was c. 3m in diameter and must have had a depth of at least 2m from the contemporary ground-surface, which had been removed in the vicinity. The filling of the pit contained bronze-working debris; it may have been dug as a quarry for the clay required for crucibles and furnace-linings.

Six graves were found which shared the same alignment, from north-west to south-east, as the Roman buildings on the site. They appear to be the vestiges of an extensive cemetery; most of the burials would have been destroyed by the later cemeteries, the graves of which had also removed many of the later Roman deposits. One grave of the earliest cemetery was found at the western corner of the site and another some 24m distant, above the street on the south-east side of the *basilica.* The other four were arranged in a row which crossed the line occupied by the south-west wall of the *basilica.* Human remains from two of these graves gave radiocarbon dates of A.D. 420±70 and 490±80, which indicates that the cemetery was established by about the middle of the fifth century.[2] The burials were made without grave-goods and, as far as could be determined, without wooden coffins. Five adults were represented, four males and a female;[3] only one corner of the sixth grave survived, and no traces of its occupant were recovered.

Various arguments in favour of the Christian character of the cemetery have been set out at length elsewhere.[4] It was succeeded by another cemetery, undoubtedly Christian, which can be associated with the monastery at Exeter where St. Boniface was educated in c. 680. Two centuries divide the date of the earlier burials and the monastery mentioned by the biographer of St. Boniface,[5] but the possibility of some connection between the two still remains: the first cemetery may have continued in use for a considerable time and the cemetery associated with the monastery may have been established well before c. 680.

These cemeteries provide a clue to events at Exeter between the end of the Roman period and the establishment of the Anglo-Saxon town in the late ninth century. The cemetery of the fifth century may have come to be associated with a religious community which was the predecessor of the monastery at which St. Boniface was educated.

Sites in other parts of the Roman town tell us scarcely anything about the period between the fifth and ninth centuries. No imported pottery from the Mediterranean, which has been found on a number of other Dark Age sites in the South-West, has come to light; indeed, there is a complete absence of finds which can be dated to this period.[6] Little is known about the demolition of the town-houses, and nothing about the date at which this took place. Where the latest Roman levels survive, they are sealed by a deposit of dark soil mixed with Roman pottery, coins and other objects (e.g. on *Insula* IV/V, site 1, *Insula* IX, site 1; see Fig. 37). The dark soil contains some building materials, but extensive spreads of the rubble which would have resulted from the demolition of the buildings have yet to be recorded. The source of the dark soil may have been partly humus which had originally accumulated over the collapsed walls of masonry structures.[7] It is clear that at some time the very considerable amounts of rubble which would have resulted from the demolition or decay of the buildings had been removed (this would certainly have been necessary when habitation of the town was resumed on an extensive scale in the later Anglo-Saxon period), and the dark soil may thus represent the debris which remained after this clearance. Certain types of pottery, both imported and local, were introduced at Exeter in the tenth or eleventh century;[8] their absence from the dark soil indicates that the clearance of rubble took place before this date.

There is a complete lack of evidence for occupation on every site at Exeter, apart from that of the *basilica* and *forum*, between a date at some time in the fifth century, very probably before the middle of that century, and the later Anglo-Saxon period; during that period urban life ceased. A thread of continuity, however, may be provided by the successive cemeteries on the site of the *basilica* and *forum;* the establishments with which these were associated could well represent an unbroken tradition of religious observances, originating in the fifth century and continued down to the present day by means of the Anglo-Saxon monastery and the later Cathedrals, both Saxo-Norman and medieval.

NOTES

1. *EAR* (i), 110–1.
2. ibid., 111.
3. See report by the late C. M. Wells in ibid., 245–50.
4. ibid., 112–3.
5. Willibald, *Vitae Sancti Bonifatii,* I (Levison, 1905, 6).
6. Shortt (1840, 79–109) records twelve Byzantine coins from Exeter, eleven from a sewer trench dug between Broadgate and Milk Lane in 1810 and one found on a building-site at South Street in 1833. On both occasions large numbers of Imperial issues from the Eastern Mediterranean were also said to have been recovered together with other coins, such as Ptolemaic issues, which are quite out of place on a Romano-British site. These motley collections of coins have been the subject of much discussion which will be reviewed by N. Shiel in a forthcoming article. It is only necessary to state here that the coins are likely to have found their way to this country in fairly recent times (p. 2).
7. The dark soil was first noted above the metalling of what is now recognised as the market-place on the south-west side of the *forum* (p. 52). 'It was a black sterile mould, 4–9 in. thick, merging imperceptibly into the medieval and recent layers. An analysis by Professor F. Zeuner showed that although it was a soil very rich in humus such as would result from the decay of vegetable matter, it also contained small particles of bone, tile, and charcoal, which might have been washed or wind-blown from rubbish-heaps nearby . . . ' (Fox 1952, 41).
8. For a consideration of the date of the earliest medieval pottery from Exeter, see J. P. Allan in *EAR* (iii), forthcoming.

GLOSSARY

A number of technical terms are employed in this book. Some occur only once and their meanings are adequately explained in the text. Others occur more frequently and it is necessary to explain them, *giving, however, only the particular sense in which they are used here.* In particular the Latin terms employed by the classical writers who describe a Roman military camp have been applied to the plan of the legionary fortress. These are most easily explained by giving a brief account of its lay-out and by reference to Fig. 7:

The defences of a legionary fortress usually form a rectangular enclosure, as at Exeter. The interior of the fortress is divided into two unequal parts by a street, the ***via principalis,*** which cuts across its width. The smaller of the parts so formed, the ***praetentura,*** is again divided by another street, the ***via praetoria,*** which meets the *via principalis* at right-angles. At the junction of the two streets stand the ***principia*** or headquarters, consisting principally of a large courtyard, one side of which is closed off by a hall behind which is a range of offices with a shrine at its centre where the legionary standards are kept. At both ends of the *via principalis* there are gates: at the left end (from the point of view of a person looking from the *principia* along the *via praetoria*) the ***porta principalis sinistra,*** and at the right end, the ***porta principalis dextra.*** Another gate, the ***porta praetoria,*** stands at the head of the *via praetoria.* The buildings which run across the middle of the fortress, bounded by the *via principalis* on one side and containing the *principia* at its centre, are the ***latera praetorii.*** The remainder of the fortress interior is termed the ***retentura;*** this is bisected by a street, the ***via decumana,*** with a gate, the ***porta decumana,*** at its head. The ***via quintana*** runs across the width of the *retentura.* The buildings within the fortress are enclosed by a street, the ***via sagularis,*** which runs around the interior of the defences, separated from them by a narrow plot, the ***intervallum.***

Aediles: a pair of magistrates appointed by the *ordo* (*s.v.*) and primarily responsible for the maintenance of public works.

Amphora: a large pottery vessel used for the transport and storage of wine, oil and other liquids.

Antefix: a plaque of baked clay decorating the eaves or gables of a roof.

Basilica and ***forum:*** the administrative and commercial centre of a town, consisting of a large courtyard or open market-place, usually closed on three sides by porticos with ranges of rooms behind, and on the fourth by the *basilica.* The latter was a large hall with a tribunal (*s.v.*) at one or both ends, and a range of rooms at the rear, housing offices, the *curia* (*s.v.*) and a shrine for the tutelary deity (*s.v.*) of the town.

Canabae: a civil settlement outside a legionary fortress.

Cantharus: a two-handled vase, often used as a decorative motif in mosaics.

Civitas peregrina: a self-governing community within the Roman Empire, membership of which, before the third century, did not in itself confer any rights of Roman citizenship.

Colonia: a settlement of legionary veterans.

Columbarium: a funerary room or vault with niches in its sides to accommodate containers for the cremated remains of the dead.

Contubernium: originally a tent containing eight men; also refers to the pair of rooms, one for storing equipment, the other for sleeping, which accommodated a unit of eight (?) men in a barrack-block.

Curia: council-chamber of the *ordo* (*s.v.*).

Decurion: a member of the *ordo (s.v.).*

Duoviri iuridicundo: the senior pair of magistrates in the *ordo* (*s.v.*).

Forum: *basilica* and *forum* (*s.v.*).

Insula: the plot of land defined by the grid-system of streets in a town.

Labrum: a water-basin supported on a pedestal in a bath-house.

Mortarium: a shallow bowl with a spout, its interior surface lined with grit (or, less commonly, scored concentrically) to assist in grinding food to a purée.

Municipium: a town with institutions established and defined by charters from the Roman government, the citizens of which received either full or modified rights of Roman citizenship.

Ordo: the governing council of a *civitas peregrina* (*s.v.*), consisting of decurions (*s.v.*), appointed on the basis of a property qualification, from amongst whom magistrates were appointed.

Oppidum: a term used by the Romans to describe large native settlements approximating in size and function to towns.

Pagus: a sub-division of a *civitas peregrina* (*s.v.*).

Piscina: pool.

Praefectus castrorum: a senior officer of a legion third in line of command, in charge of the fortress and the technical services of the legion.

Samian: red-coated pottery used as tableware and frequently decorated with elaborate moulded designs.

Terminus ante quem, terminus post quem: in archaeological stratigraphy, the date before which (*ante quem*) or after which (*post quem*) a deposit was laid down, building constructed, etc.

Terrazzo: a mortar floor into the surface of which pebbles or fragments of marble have been pressed; when dry, the floor is ground down to produce a smooth surface.

Tesserae: small cubes of stone, pottery, glass, etc., used to build up a mosaic or tessellated floor.

Tribunal: a platform for a magistrate.

Tutelary deity: the diety personifying and protecting the town.

Vicus: a small settlement or a division of a town permitted to appoint its own magistrates.

BIBLIOGRAPHY

This bibliography does not include reviews and annual summaries such as Roman Britain in 19..; these are cited in the chapter-notes by means of the appropriate volume and page numbers.

Abbott, F.F. and Johnson, A.C. (1926) *Municipal Administration in the Roman Empire*, Princeton.

AE *L'Année Epigraphique* (published in *Revue Archéologique*).

Alföldy, G. (1968) *Die Hilfstruppen der römischen Provinz Germania Inferior*, Dusseldorf.

Aylwin Cotton, M. (1947) 'Excavations at Silchester, 1938-9', *Archaeologia*, **92**, 121-67.

Barrett, A. A. (1979) 'The Career of Cogidubnus', *Britannia*, **10**, 227-42.

Beavis, J. (1970) 'Some Aspects of the Use of Purbeck Marble in Roman Britain', *Proc. Dorset Natur. Hist. Archaeol. Soc.*, **92**, 181-204.

Behrens, G. (1917-18) 'Neue und ältere Funde aus dem Legionskastell Mainz', *Mainzer Zeitschrift*, **12-13**, 21-46.

Biddle, M. (1970) 'Excavations at Winchester, 1969: Eighth Interim Report', *Antiq. J.*, **50**, 277-326.

Bidwell, P. T. and Boon, G. C. (1976) 'An Antefix Type of the Second Augustan Legion from Exeter', *Britannia*, **7**, 278-80.

Bidwell, P. T., Bridgwater, R. and Silvester, R. J. (1979) 'The Roman Fort at Okehampton, Devon', *Britannia*, **10**, 255-8.

Birley, E. (1952) 'Roman Garrisons in Wales', *Archaeol. Cambrensis*, **102**, 9-19.

Birley, E. (1953) *Roman Britain and the Roman Army*, Kendal.

Birley, A. (1979) *The People of Roman Britain*.

Blagg, T. F. C. (1979) 'The Date of the Temple at Bath', *Britannia*, **10**, 101-7.

Bogaers, J. E. and Haalebos, J. K. (1977) 'Die Nijmegener Legionslager seit 70 nach Christus' in *Studien zu den Militärgrenzen Roms*, II (pp. 93-108), Cologne.

Boon,. G. C. (1969) 'Belgic and Roman Silchester: The Excavations of 1954-8 with an Excursus on the Early History of Calleva', *Archaeologia*, **102**, 1-82.

Boon, G. C. (1972) *Isca, the Roman Legionary Fortress at Caerleon, Mon.*, Cardiff.

Boon, G. C. (1974) *Silchester, the Roman Town of Calleva*, Newton Abbot.

Brailsford, J. W. (1962) *Hod Hill, volume one: Antiquities from Hod Hill in the Durden Collection*.

Branigan, K. (1974) 'Vespasian and the South-West', *Proc. Dorset Natur. Hist. Archaeol. Soc.*, **96**, 50-7.

Breeze, D. J. and Dobson, B. (1974) 'Fort Types as a Guide to Garrisons: A Reconsideration', in (Eds.) Birley, E., Dobson, B. and Jarrett, M., *Roman Frontier Studies 1969* (pp. 13-19), Cardiff.

Burrow, I. (1978) 'The Town Defences of Exeter', *Rep. Trans. Devon Ass.*, **109**, 13-40.

Casson, L. (1971) *Ships and Seamanship in the Ancient World*, Princeton.

Charlesworth, D. (1971) 'The Defences of Isurium Brigantum', in (Ed.) Butler, R.M., *Soldier and Civilian in Roman Yorkshire* (pp. 155-64), Leicester.

CIL *Corpus Inscriptionum Latinarum*, Berlin, 1863-.

Clifford, E.M. (1955) 'Stamped Tiles Found in Gloucestershire', *J. Roman Stud.*, **45**, 69-72.

Collingwood, R. G. and Richmond, I. A. (1969) *The Archaeology of Roman Britain*.

Corder, P. (1951) *The Roman Town and Villa at Great Casterton, Rutland . . . .*,Nottingham.

Corder, P. (1954) *The Roman Town and Villa at Great Casterton, Rutland, 2nd interim report for the years 1950-53*, Nottingham.

Corder, P. (1961) *The Roman Town and Villa at Great Casterton, Rutland, 3rd interim report for 1954-58*, Nottingham.

Crummy, P. (1977) 'Colchester, Fortress and Colonia', *Britannia*, **8**, 65-106.

Cunliffe, B. (Ed.) (1968) *Fifth Report on the Excavations of the Roman Fort at Richborough, Kent*.

Cunliffe, B. (1969) *Roman Bath*.

Darling, M. (1977) 'Pottery from Early Military Sites in Roman Britain' in (Eds.) Dore, J. and Greene, K. T., *Roman Pottery Studies in Britain and Beyond* (pp. 57-100), Oxford.

Douch, H. L. and Beard, S. W. (1970) 'Excavations at Carvossa, Probus, 1968-70: Interim Report', *Cornish Archaeol.*, **9**, 93-7.

EAR (i) *Exeter Archaeological Reports, Vol. I:* Bidwell, P. T., *The Legionary Bath-House and Basilica and Forum at Exeter*, Exeter, 1979.

EAR (ii) *Exeter Archaeological Reports, Vol. II:* Maltby, M., *Faunal Studies on Urban Sites: The Animal Bones from Exeter, 1971–5,* Sheffield, 1979.

EAR (iii) *Exeter Archaeological Reports, Vol. III:* Allan, J. P., *Medieval and Post-Medieval Finds from Exeter,* forthcoming.

EAR (iv) *Exeter Archaeological Reports, Vol. IV:* Bidwell, P. T., *Excavations on Roman Sites in Exeter, 1971–80: The Finds,* forthcoming.

Eicholz, D. E. (1972) 'How long did Vespasian serve in Britain', *Britannia,* **3**, 149–63.

Elkington, D. (1976) 'The Mendip Lead Industry', in (Eds.) Branigan, K. and Fowler, P. J., *The Roman West Country* (pp. 183–97), Newton Abbot.

Ettlinger, E. (1972) 'Berichte über das Symposium zum 75 jährigen Jubiläum der Gesellschaft Pro Vindonissa', *Jahresberichte der Gesellschaft Pro Vindonissa 1972,* 14–20.

Farrar, R. A. H. (1965) 'A Romano-British Rider Relief from Whitcombe', *Proc. Dorset Natur. Hist. Archaeol. Soc.,* **86**, 103–4.

Farrar, R. A. H. (1973) 'The Techniques and Sources of Romano-British black-burnished Ware', in (Ed.) Detsicas, A., *Current Research in Romano-British Coarse Pottery* (pp. 67–103).

Fellmann, R. (1958) *Die Principia des Legionslagers Vindonissa und das Zentralgebäude der römischer Lager und Kastelle,* Brugg.

Fentress, E. (1979) *Numidia and the Roman Army,* Oxford.

Fox, A. (1952) *Roman Exeter (Isca Dumnoniorum): Excavations in the War-damaged Areas, 1945–7,* Manchester.

Fox, A. (1952a) 'Roman Discoveries in Exeter, 1951–2', *Proc. Devon Archaeol. Soc.,* **10**, 106–114.

Fox, A. (1966) 'Roman Exeter *(Isca Dumnoniorum),* Origins and Early Development' in (Ed.) Wacher, J. S., *The Civitas Capitals of Roman Britain* (pp. 46–51), Leicester.

Fox, A. (1968) 'Excavations at the South Gate, Exeter, 1964–5', *Proc. Devon Archaeol. Soc.,* **26**, 1–20.

Fox, A. (1973) *South-West England* (revised edn.), Newton Abbot.

Fox, A. (1974) 'New Light on the Military Occupation of South-West England' in (Eds.) Birley, E., Dobson, B. and Jarrett, M., *Roman Frontier Studies* 1969, Cardiff.

Fox, A. and Ravenhill, W. (1959) 'The Stoke Hill Roman Signal Station, Excavations 1956–7', *Rep. Trans. Devon Ass.,* **91**, 71–82.

Fox, A. and Ravenhill, W. (1966) 'Early Roman Outposts on the North Devon Coast, Old Burrow and Martinhoe', *Proc. Devon Archaeol. Explor. Soc.,* **24**, 3–39.

Fox, A. and Ravenhill, W. (1972) 'The Roman Fort at Nanstallon, Cornwall', *Britannia,* **3**, 56–111.

Frere, S. S. (1962) 'Excavations at Dorchester-on-Thames', *Archaeol. J.,* **119**, 114–50.

Frere, S. S. (1964) 'Verulamium, Three Roman Cities', *Antiquity,* **38**, 103–12.

Frere, S. S. (1967) *Britannia.*

Frere, S. S. (1972) *Verulamium Excavations: I.*

Frere, S. S. (1978) *Britannia* (revised edn.).

Frere, S. S. and St. Joseph, J. K. (1974) 'The Roman Fortress at Longthorpe', *Britannia,* **5**, 1–129.

von Gonzenbach, V. (1976) 'Ein Heiligtum im Legionslager Vindonissa' in (Eds.) Bögli, H. and Martin, C., *Mélanges d'Histoiré Ancienne et d'Archéologie offerts à Paul Collart (Cahiers d'Archéologie, No. 5)* (pp. 205–21), Lausanne.

Goodchild, R. G. (1946) *Roman Exeter (The City of Isca Dumnoniorum),* privately printed.

Goodchild, R. G. (1947) 'An Antiquary in Devon (W. T. P. Shortt, 1800–1881)', *Rep. Trans. Devon Ass.,* **79**, 229–55.

Gough, R. (1806) Translation of W. Camden's *Britannia.*

Green, M. J. (1976) *The Religions of Civilian Roman Britain,* Oxford.

Greene, K. T. (1973) 'The Pottery from Usk' in (Ed.) Detsicas, A., *Current Research in Romano-British Coarse Pottery* (pp. 25–37).

Greenfield, E. (1964) 'Excavations of a Bombed Site in Chapel St., Exeter', *Rep. Trans. Devon Ass.,* **96**, 339–79.

Griffiths, M. (1974) 'Recent Work by the Exeter Archaeological Field Unit', *Proc. Devon Archaeol. Soc.,* **32**, 167–70.

Griffiths, N. A. (1978) 'A Fragment of a Roman Cavalry Tombstone from Cirencester', *Britannia,* **9**, 396–7.

Harris, E. and Harris, J. R. (1965) *The Oriental Cults in Britain,* Leiden.

Harte, W.J., Schoppe, J.W. and Tapley-Soper, H (Eds.) (1947) John Vowell *alias* Hoker's *The Description of the Citie of Exeter* (3 vols.), Exeter.

Hassall, M. W. C. and Rhodes, J. (1974) 'Excavations at the new Market Hall, Gloucester, 1966–7', *Trans. Bristol Gloucestershire Archaeol. Soc.,* **93,** 15–100.

Holmes, J. (1962) 'The Defences of Roman Chichester', *Sussex Archaeol. Colln.,* **100,** 80–93.

Hoskins, W. G. (1960) *Two Thousand Years in Exeter,* Exeter.

Hull, M. R. (1958) *Roman Colchester,* Oxford.

Hurst, H. (1972) 'Excavations at Gloucester 1968–71: First Interim Report', *Antiq. J.,* **52,** 24–69.

Hurst, H. (1975) 'Excavations at Gloucester, Third Interim Report: Kingsholm 1966–1975', *Antiq. J.,* **55,** 267–94.

Hurst, H. (1976) 'Gloucester (Glevum); A *Colonia* in the West Country' in (Eds.) Branigan, K. and Fowler, P. J., *The Roman West Country* (pp. 63–80), Newton Abbot.

Jackson, A. M. (1972) 'Medieval Exeter, the Exe and the Earldom of Devon', *Rep. Trans. Devon Ass.,* **104,** 57–81.

Jarrett, M. G. (1968) '*Legio XX Valeria Victrix* in Britain', *Archaeol. Cambrensis,* **117,** 77–91.

Jarvis, K. (1976) 'The M5 Motorway and the Peamore/Pocombe Link', *Proc. Devon Archaeol. Soc.,* **34,** 41–72.

Jarvis, K. and Maxfield, V. A. (1975) 'The Excavation of a First-Century Roman Farmstead and a Late Neolithic Settlement, Topsham, Devon', *Proc. Devon Archaeol. Soc.,* **33,** 209–66.

Kenyon, K. M. (1935) 'The Roman Theatre at Verulamium, St. Albans', *Archaeologia,* **84,** 213–81.

King, A. C. (1978) 'A Roman Marching Camp near Tiverton', *Proc. Devon Archaeol. Soc.,* **36,** 254–6.

Kropatschek, G. (1909) 'Ausgrabungen bei Haltern: Die Fundstücke der Jahre 1905 bis 1907', *Mitteilungen altertümer Kommission Westfalen,* **5,** 323–75.

Laur-Belart, R. (1933) 'Grabungen der Gesellschaft Pro Vindonissa im Jahre 1932', *Anzeiger für Schweizerische Altertumskunde,* **35,** 1–16.

Laur-Belart, R. (1935) *Vindonissa, Lager und Vicus (Römisch-germanische Forschungen, 10).*

Leland's *Itinerary,* (Ed.) Smith, L. T., London, 1907.

Levison, W. (Ed.) (1905) *Vitae Sancti Bonifatii,* Hanover.

Manning, W.H. (1975) 'Roman Military Timber Granaries in Britain', *Saalburg Jahrbuch,* **32,** 105–29.

Manning, W. H. (1976) 'The Conquest of the West Country', in (Eds.) Branigan, K. and Fowler, P. J., *The Roman West Country* (pp. 15–41), Newton Abbot.

Manning, W. H. (1978) 'Usk, Roman Legionary Fortress', *Curr. Archaeol.,* No. 62, 71–7.

Margary, I. D. (1967) *Roman Roads in Britain.*

Maxfield, V. A. (1980) 'The Roman Military Occupation of South-West England: Further Light and Fresh Problems' in (Eds.) Hanson, W. S. and Keppie, L. F. J., *Roman Frontier Studies 1979, Papers presented to the 12th International Congress of Roman Frontier Studies* (pp. 297–309), Oxford.

Miles, H. (1975) 'Excavations at Woodbury Castle, East Devon, 1971', *Proc. Devon Archaeol. Soc.,* **33,** 183–208.

Miles, H. (1977) 'The Honeyditches Villa, Seaton', *Britannia,* **8,** 107–48.

Milles, J. (1782) 'Account of some Roman Antiquities discovered at Exeter', *Archaeologia,* **6,** 1–5.

Mócsy, A. (1974) *Pannonia and Upper Moesia.*

Montague, L. A. D. and Morris, P. (1933–6) 'Report of the Exeter Excavation Committee: Roman Remains in the Cathedral Close, Exeter', *Proc. Devon Archaeol. Explor. Soc.,* **2,** 224–37.

Montgomerie-Neilson, E. and Montague, L. A. D. (1933–6) 'Reports of the Exeter Excavation Committee', *Proc. Devon Archaeol. Explor. Soc.,* **2,** 53–103, 124–30.

Morris, P. (1933–6) 'Report of the Exeter Excavation Committee', *Proc. Devon Archaeol. Explor. Soc.,* **2,** 227–31.

Morris, P., Montague, L. A. D. and Ralegh Radford, C. A. (1937–47) 'Report of the Exeter Excavation Committee', *Proc. Devon Archaeol. Explor. Soc.,* **3,** 136–41.

Musgrave, W. (1719) *Belgium Britannicum,* Exeter.

Myers, J. N. L., Steer, K. A. and Chitty, A. M. H. (1959) 'The Defences of Isurium Brigantum (Aldborough)', *Yorkshire Archaeol. J.,* **40,** 1–78.

Nash-Williams, V. E. (1929–32) 'The Problem of Roman Exeter', *Proc. Devon Archaeol. Explor. Soc.,* **1,** 8–9.

Nash-Williams, V. E. (1930) 'Further Excavations at Caerwent, Monmouthshire, 1923–5', *Archaeologia,* **80,** 229–288.

Newton, R. (1968) *Victorian Exeter, 1837–1914,* Leicester.

Ogilvie, R.M. and Richmond, I.A. (Eds.) (1967) *Cornelii Taciti, De Vita Agricolae,* Oxford.

Oldenstein, J. (1976) 'Zur Ausrüstung römischer Auxiliareinheiten', *Bericht der Römisch-Germanischen Kommission,* **57,** 49–284.

Oliver, G. and Jones, P. (Eds.) (1845) *Westcote's A View of Devonshire in 1630 . . . ,* Exeter.

O'Neill, B. H. St. J. (1934) 'The Roman Villa at Magor Farm, near Camborne, Cornwall', *J. Brit. Archaeol. Ass.,* **39,** 117–75.

Peers, R. N. R. and Wright, R. P. (1965) 'A Roman Altar in Godmanston Church', *Proc. Dorset Natur. Hist. Archaeol. Soc.,* **86,** 104–6.

Petch, D. F. (1962) 'Excavations at Lincoln, 1955–58', *Archaeol. J.,* **117,** 40–70.

von Petrikovits, H. (1968) 'Aquae Iasae', *Archeolovski Vestnik,* **19,** 89–93.

von Petrikovits, H. (1974) 'Römisches Militärhandwerk: Archäologische Forschungen der letzten Jahre', *Anzeiger der Österreichischen Akademie der Wissenschaften (Philosophisch-Historische Klasse),* **111,** 1–21.

von Petrikovits, H. (1975) *Die Innenbauten römischer Legionslager während der Prinzipatszeit,* Opladen.

Phillips, E. J. (1978) 'The Gloucester Roman Antefix: An Interpretation', *Trans. Bristol Gloucestershire Archaeol. Soc.,* **96,** 74–7.

Philp, B. J. (1977) 'The Forum of Roman London, 1968–9', *Britannia,* **8,** 1–64.

Pollard, S. (1974) 'A Late Iron Age Settlement and a Romano-British Villa at Holcombe, near Uplyme, Devon', *Proc. Devon Archaeol. Soc.,* **32,** 59–161.

Ralegh Radford, C. A. (1937–47) 'Report of the Exeter Excavation Committee: The Roman Site at Topsham', *Proc. Devon Archaeol. Soc.,* **3,** 5–23.

Ralegh Radford, C. A. and Morris, P. (1933–6) 'Report of the Exeter Excavation Committee: The Defences of Roman Exeter', *Proc. Devon Archaeol. Explor. Soc.,* **2,** 181–7.

Ralegh Radford, C. A. and Morris, P. (1933–6a) 'Report of the Exeter Excavation Committee: The Examination of the City Wall beside Trinity Street', *Proc. Devon Archaeol. Explor. Soc.,* **2,** 238–40.

RCHM Royal Commission on Historical Monuments.

Rhodes, J. F. (1964) *Catalogue of the Romano-British Sculptures in the Gloucester City Museum,* Gloucester.

RIB (i) Collingwood, R. G. and Wright, R. P., *The Roman Inscriptions of Britain: I, Inscriptions on Stone,* Oxford, 1965.

Richmond, I. A. (1968) *Hod Hill, volume 2: Excavations carried out between 1951 and 1958.*

Richmond, I. A. and Crawford, O. G. S. (1949) 'The British Section of the Ravenna Cosmography', *Archaeologia,* **93,** 1–50.

Rigold, S. E. (1954) 'Totnes Castle: Recent Excavations by the Ancient Mons. Dept.', *Rep. Trans. Devon Ass.,* **86,** 228–257.

Rivet, A. L. F. (1970) 'The British Section of the Antonine Itinerary', *Britannia,* **1,** 34–82.

Rivet, A. L. F. (1974) 'Some Aspects of Ptolemy's Geography of Britain' in (Ed.) Chevallier, R., *Littérature Gréco-Romaine et Géographie Historique (Mélanges offerts à Roger Dion)* (pp. 55–81), Paris.

Rivet, A. L. F. (1977) 'The Origins of Cities in Roman Britain' in (Eds.) Duval, P. M. and Frézouls, E., *Thèmes de Recherches sur les Villes Antiques d'Occident* (pp. 161–72), Paris.

Rivet, A. L. F. and Smith, C. (1979) *The Place Names of Roman Britain.*

Saxer, R. (1967) *Epigraphische Studien,* **1,** Böhlan Verlag Köln Graz.

von Schnurbein, S. (1974) *Die römischen Militäranlagen bei Haltern,* Münster.

Shiel, N. (1978) 'Two Recent Coin Hoards from Exeter', *Proc. Devon Archaeol. Soc.,* **36,** 256–8.

Shortt, W. T. P. (1840) *Sylva Antiqua Iscana.*

Shortt, W. T. P. (1841) *Collectanea Curiosa Antiqua Dumnonia.*

Silvester, R. J. (1978) 'Cropmark Sites at North Tawton and Alverdiscott', *Proc. Devon Archaeol. Soc.,* **36,** 249–54.

Silvester, R. J. (forthcoming) 'Report on Excavations on the Roman Site at Seaton', *Proc. Devon Archaeol. Soc.*

Simonett, C. (1934) 'Grabungen der Gesellschaft Pro Vindonissa im Jahre 1933', *Anzeiger für Schweizerische Altertumskunde,* **36,** 73–104.

Simonett, C. (1936) 'Grabungen der Gesellschaft Pro Vindonissa in den Jahren 1934 und 1935 auf der Breite', *Anzeiger für Schweizerische Altertumskunde,* **38,** 161–73.

Stevens, C. E. (1927) 'Ancient Writers on Britain', *Antiquity,* **1,** 189–96.

St. Joseph, J.K. (1958) 'Air Reconnaissance in Britain, 1955–7, *J. Roman Stud.,* **48,** 86–101.

Stukeley, W. (1724) *Itinerarium Curiosum.*

Thomas, C. (1964) 'Settlement history in Early Cornwall: I, The Hundreds', *Cornish Archaeol.,* **3,** 70–80.

Thomas, C. (1966) 'The character and origins of Roman Dumnonia' in (Ed.) idem., *Rural Settlement in Roman Britain* (pp. 74–98).

Thomas, J. W. (1875) *Reminiscences of Methodism in Exeter,* Exeter.

Thorpe, L. (1966) Geoffrey of Monmouth's *The History of the Kings of Britain* (Eng. trans.).

Todd, M. (1969) 'The Roman Settlement at Margidunum: the excavations of 1966–8', *Trans. Thoroton Soc. Nottinghamshire,* **78.**

Tomašević, T. (1963) 'Ausgrabung Königsfelden 1963', *Jahresberichte der Gesellschaft Pro Vindonissa,* pp. 15–24.

Toynbee, J. M. C. (1964) *Art in Britain under the Romans,* Oxford.

Ulbert, G. (1968) *Römische Waffen des 1.Jahrhunderts n.Chr.,* Stuttgart.

Ulbert, G. (1969) *Das Frührömische Kastell Rheingönheim,* Berlin.

Ulbert, G. (1970) *Das römische Donau-Kastell Risstissen, Teil 1: Die Funde aus Metall, Horn und Knochen (Urkunde zur Vor- und Frühgeschichte aus Südwürttemburg-Hohenzollern, Heft 4),* Stuttgart.

VCH Victoria County History.

Wacher, J. S. (1961) 'Cirencester 1960: First Interim Report', *Antiq. J.,* **41,** 63–71.

Wacher, J. S. (1962) 'Cirencester 1961: Second Interim Report', *Antiq. J.,* **42,** 1–14.

Wacher, J. S. (1964) 'Cirencester 1963: Fourth Interim Report', *Antiq. J.,* **44,** 9–19.

Wacher, J. S. (1974) *The Towns of Roman Britain.*

Walthew, C. V. (1975) 'The Town House and Villa House in Roman Britain', *Britannia,* **6,** 189–205.

Ward, J. (1903) *The Roman Fort of Gellygaer.*

Ward, J. (1916) 'The Fortifications of Roman Caerwent', *Archaeol. Cambrensis,* **16,** 1–36.

Webster, G. (1955–7) 'Excavations on the defences of the Romano-British Town at Kenchester 1956', *Trans. Woolhope Natur. Fld. Club,* **35,** 138–146.

Webster, G. (1959) 'An Excavation at Nunnington Park near Wiveliscombe, Somerset', *Proc. Somerset Archaeol. Natur. Hist. Soc.,* **103,** 81–91.

Webster, G. (1960) 'The Discovery of a Roman Fort at Waddon Hill, Stoke Abbott, 1969', *Proc. Dorset Natur. Hist. Archaeol. Soc.,* **82,** 88–108.

Webster, G. (1966) 'Fort and Town in early Roman Britain' in (Ed.) Wacher, J. S., *The Civitas Capitals of Roman Britain* (pp. 31–45), Leicester.

Webster, G. (1969) *The Roman Imperial Army.*

Webster, G. (1970) 'The Military Situation in Britain between A.D. 43 and 71', *Britannia,* **1,** 179–97.

Wilkes, J. J. (1969) *Dalmatia.*

Williams, M.E. (1940) 'Roman Exeter and Alexandria', *Bulletin de la Société Royale d' Archéologie d'Alexandrie,* **34,** 3–5.

Williams, J. H. (1971) 'Roman Building Materials', *Trans. Bristol Gloucestershire Archaeol. Soc.,* **90,** 95–120.

Williams, J.H. (1971) 'Roman Building-Materials in South-East England', *Britannia,* **2,** 166–95.

Wilson, D.R. (1977) 'A First-Century Fort near Gosbecks', *Britannia,* **2,** 166–95.

Worth, R. N. (1891) 'President's Address: Roman Devon', *Rep. Trans. Devon Ass.,* **23,** 25–101.

Young, C. J. (1975) 'The Defences of Roman Alchester', *Oxoniensia,* **40,** 136–171.

INDEX